PENGUIN HANDBOOKS PH71
Delphiniums
RONALD C. PARRETT

Ronald Parrett is a Cornishman, born at Truro in 1904. He was educated at Truro Cathedral School, whence he entered the service of the then Anglo-Persian Oil Company as an accountant. On his return from Persia in 1932 he joined the staff of Beaverbrook Newspapers and has held the post of chief accountant to the group for the past thirty years.

He devoted most of his spare time to cricket, football, fives, squash, tennis, and golf as a young man, and his interest in gardening did not begin until 1938. Since then his main hobby has been horticulture generally, and he has specialized in the delphinium for over twenty years. The small garden he designed and made at Cobham has been open to the public many times in the delphinium season, and he pioneered the first six Year Books which helped to restore the fallen fortunes of the British Delphinium Society from 1953 onwards.

Ronald Parrett recalls that his first interest in delphiniums followed a chance visit to some trials at Wisley in 1940. Since then his own introductions – 'Daily Express', 'Sunday Express', and 'Evening Standard' – have all gained Awards of Merit, and many other attractive varieties are currently being introduced by him.

The cover illustration is of delphiniums 'Basil Clitheroe' (Highly Commended, 1961) and 'Blue Pearl' in the author's garden

The public interest in the modern delphinium as evidenced in the author's garden, open annually in aid of the National Gardens Scheme

RONALD C. PARRETT

DELPHINIUMS

Prepared in conjunction and collaboration
with The Royal Horticultural Society

PENGUIN BOOKS

Penguin Books Ltd, Harmondsworth, Middlesex
U.S.A. : Penguin Books Inc., 3300 Clipper Mill Road, Baltimore 11, Md
AUSTRALIA : Penguin Books Pty Ltd, 762 Whitehorse Road,
Mitcham, Victoria

—

First   published 1961

—

Copyright © Ronald C. Parrett, 1961

—

Made and printed in Great Britain
by Jarrold & Sons Ltd, Norwich

Contents

List of Plates

9

Author's Preface

In compiling this handbook my objective has been two-fold – first, to show the evolution of the modern *elatum* hybrid out of the mountain species, and secondly, to present the cultivation of the plant in all its aspects in such a detailed and reasoned manner as to give an adequate and convincing answer to all the doubts and queries which can arise.

The delphinium is a plant for which I have a very real affection and which I have known intimately for many years, and the fulfilment of the task accorded to me by the Council of the Royal Horticultural Society has afforded me a great deal of pleasure and satisfaction.

As the bibliography relative to the delphinium is insignificant compared with other genera I have done my best to make this book as complete and up-to-date as possible. All sources of information have been utilized and I am grateful to numerous persons for assistance given. Special thanks are due to those delphinium lovers Mr Frank Reinelt of California and Mr James Baker of Codsall for their help, so generously given, in relation to the Giant Pacific and Bishop strains respectively.

My greatest debt is to Mr Allan G. Langdon, V.M.H., and to his son, Dr Brian J. Langdon, without whose help this book would definitely have been very much the poorer. Mr Allan Langdon is, of course, the doyen of the delphinium world; his knowledge of the plant is unrivalled and I was indeed fortunate to be able to confer with him freely at all times. His response was always generous and unfailing and I wish to record, with affection, my appreciation of all the invaluable assistance he gave me.

There remains to thank Mr Arthur Hunt, who so generously gave me week-end after week-end of his leisure and showed such endless patience and skill in assembling the pictorial history of the modern hybrid at all its stages.

While nothing can be perfect, I feel fairly confident that the effort made results in a book which will be of interest and instruction to many in the pursuit of better and better delphiniums, and I am grateful to the Royal Horticultural Society for honouring me with the authorship.

R. C. P.

Cobham
19 April 1961

1 · The history of the modern delphinium

The Past

Almost two thousand years ago a Greek, by name Pedanios Dioscorides, who served in the army of the Emperor Nero and was thus a contemporary of the Roman historian Pliny, established medical botany for the first time by compiling the manuscript of his *Materia Medica*, a work in which the medicinal properties of about 600 plants were amply described. This encyclopedia remained standard for fifteen centuries, and was important enough to be translated into English by John Goodyer in 1652, whose manuscript of 4,540 pages remained unpublished until 1934. The original Greek manuscript of Dioscorides is in the Vienna State Library. Lovers of the delphinium will be interested to know that in this medical work are the first recorded mentions of the plant's ancestors, but will possibly be shocked to learn of the use to which the plant was put, as for instance in these quotations from Goodyer's translation:

The seed in the cods which drank in wine helpeth the scorpion-bitten as nothing else. They also say that scorpions grow faint and become unactive and benumbed, the herb being put to them....

Staphis agria ... the seed in the little cods green.... But that within white, sharp to the taster. If any give ten or fifteen grains of this, having beaten it in melicrate, it purgeth thick stuff by vomitings, but let them walk which have drunk it.

This particular wild delphinium, *D. staphisagria*, was also described by Pliny who stated that the powdered seeds killed lice on the head and elsewhere. It is interesting to note that two thousand years later the sap of the modern hybrids blackens and erodes the skin of the fingers if a few hundred cuttings are taken. The old Latin name was, significantly, *herba pedicularis*, but there were many other synonyms also which clearly indicate that this family of plants was spread through Southern and Western Europe, parts of Africa, Asia Minor, and Persia. The Greek name for the plant means literally 'wild raisin', the foliage being similar to that of the wild vine.

1. (*left*) 'Royal Marine' is one of the most impressive of modern named varieties. Its three spikes of bloom are of an intense pure violet, and the formation and habit are excellent

2. (*right*) This pleasing plum-purple with the frilled petals is 'Savrola', by Blackmore & Langdon

In Dioscorides' work two wild delphiniums were described and illustrated, but in fact it is now known that at least fifteen species abound in Greece, the Aegean Islands, and in Asia Minor alone. One of these is *D. peregrinum*, the unopened buds of which faintly resemble a dolphin in miniature, thus inspiring the Latinized name *Delphinium*, from the Greek 'a little dolphin'. Dioscorides's plants, and the others referred to, together with some few hundred other species which have since been discovered the world over, probably all existed long before his time. Their natural habitat, where large stands of the widely differing varieties may be found, has remained largely unchanged. Living, as they do, in almost standard conditions on the slopes of mountain valleys as widely separated as the Balkans, Asia Minor, Afghanistan, Western America, China, Siberia, Abyssinia, Europe, and East Africa, there is no reason to suppose that they have not done so for thousands of years. In the spring of 328 B.C., when

Alexander the Great crossed the Hindu Kush to conquer Afghanistan and North West India, the mountain strongholds he systematically reduced were sited where the villages of today still stand. It is likely that they found natural stands of the golden yellow *D. zalil* both in the high lands of North East Persia as well as North Western Afghanistan, for this plant has for centuries provided the dye for dyeing silk in these parts and still does so today.

Of all the hundreds of wild delphiniums none is indigenous to Great Britain except *D. ajacis*, the forerunner of our annual larkspurs, and no perennial types were in garden cultivation anywhere until the eighteenth century when the French firm of Vilmorin, Andrieux, offered seed of *D. elatum*. This particular wild delphinium is generally accepted as the principal forebear of the present-day semi-double hybrid delphiniums and that is why they are generally referred to as *elatum* delphiniums. *D. elatum*, the type plant, is widely distributed from the Pyrenees to Siberia; in the wild it grows from 4 ft to 6 ft in height and bears half-inch single-petalled florets of cornflower blue, with a darker blue and yellow-bearded eye, set close together on slender stems. Seed of this plant began to be cultivated more widely in France, together with seed of other single-petalled wildings such as the violet-blue *D. formosum* and rich blue *D. grandiflorum*. As with most seed collected in the wild, results would be uniform within limits. Undoubtedly, better forms emerged from the cultivated plants and the elimination of all unsatisfactory plants gradually created improved standards. Natural hybrids between improved forms of *D. elatum* and *D. formosum* may well have occurred since both have the same chromosome count which indicates the possibility of inter-crossing. One form appeared in England in 1837 and was called *D. barlowi*, being grown by a Mr Barlow of Manchester; this was a rich blue and the florets were semi-double, not single. It was said to be a hybrid from *D. grandiflorum*.

For the most part nurserymen seemed content to leave matters as they were until midway through the nineteenth century when M. Victor Lemoine of Nancy took the first steps which led eventually to the magnificent garden plants we have today. In front of me as I write is Lemoine's eighteenth annual list, dated Autumn 1857, in which he offered no less than seventeen hybrid

15

3. 'Silver Moon' is perhaps the loveliest of all the silvery mauves
grown at Bath – a plant which will grow well for any gardener

COLLECTION DE DELPHINIUMS VIVACES.

PRIX.

Alphonse Karr (*Richalet*).... » »
Barlowi versicolor (*V. H.*);
fleurs doubles, très-larges,
belle couleur du type, pana-
chée de tons métalliques, une
des plus belles et des plus ri-
ches variétés.............. 2 »
Bellidiflorum (*L.*).......... 1 »
Cheirantiflorum superbum
(*Lemoine*).............. » 50
C. Glijm (*Lemoine*); fleurs grandes, forme parfaite, très-pleines, circonférence bleu foncé;
au centre rosace bleue et blanche, mêlée de tons verdâtres,
variété de premier ordre.... 1 25
Claire Courant (*Courant*), fl.
pl. bleu azuré brillant à fond
blanc................... 10 »
Docteur Andry (*Richalet*) ... 2 »
Elegans (*L.*).............. » 50
Félix Poulet (*Rend.*)........ » 50
Formosum cel stinum (*Thib.
et Ket.*)................ » 50
Hébé.................... » 60
* **Hendersoni**.............. » 50
— 6 plantes................ 2 »
* — **Ligeri** (*Liger*); fleurs plus
grandes, mieux étoffées que le
type, bleu violet foncé, à re-
flets veloutés............ » 60
— 6 plantes................ 2 50
Hermann Stenger (*L.*)...... » 50
Hyacintiflorum plenum.... » 50
Keteleeri (*Lemoine*); rameaux
serrés, fleurs de première
grandeur bleu de ciel clair, à
mouche blanche, taille de 1 m.
50 y compris le rameau floral. 3 »
Mᵐᵉ Grisau (*L.*).......... » 50
* — **Guichard** (*Rougier*)..... » 50
— **Henri-Jacotot** (*Lemoine*);
longs rameaux de grandes

PRIX.

fleurs doubles, belle couleur
bleu turquoise, nuance nou-
velle et éclatante; une des plus
belles variétés connues..... 1 25
— — 6 plantes.............. 5 »
— **Paillet** (*Courant*)........ 1 »
— **Pelé** (*Lemoine*).......... » 50
— **Thibaut** (*Lemoine*); fleurs
pleines, rose lilas tèndre.... » 75
* **Magnificum**............. » 50
M. Barthère (*L.*).......... » 60
— — 6 plantes............. 2 50
— **Duchartre** (*Lemoine*)..... 1 25
— **Le Bihan** (*L.*); fleurs doubles, très-grandes, violet foncé, rameaux compactes..... 1 25
— **Rouillard** (*Lemoine*); lilas
clair transparent, mouche bru-
ne, fleurs grandes et doubles. » 60
— — 6 plantes............. 2 50
* **Montmorency**........... » 75
* **Morei**.................. » 50
Palmerston (*Lemoine*); fleurs
moyennes, extra-pleines, en
forme de renoncule, blanc ro-
sé bordé lilas, pointé jaunâtre 2 50
Paul et Virginie (*Lemoine*);
fleurs de moyenne grandeur,
très-pleines, bleu brillant; le
centre composé de plus de 20
pétales blanc de neige ligné
bleu.................... 4 »
Perfectum fl. pl........... » 50
Pompon de Tirlemont (*Van
Houtte*).................. 1 »
Psyché (*L.*).............. » 75
Ranunculæflorum (*Lemoine*);
taille moyenne, fleurs très-pleines, bleu de cobalt, base des
pétales blanc ; l'une des plus
brillantes et des meilleures
variétés.................. » 60
— 6 plantes................ 2 50

17

DELPHINIUMS A FLEURS PLEINES.

Obs. — Il est de notoriété, que les Delphiniums ne sont dans leur beauté, que dès la deuxième année de leur mise en place.

HERMANN STENGER; fleurs tr.-gr., tr.-doubles, très-bien faites, le centre de chaque pétale est rose satiné lilas, les bords sont bleu de ciel très-foncé; les fleurs garnissent bien les rameaux, la plante est très-vigoureuse et produit beaucoup d'effet.

Livrable en bons sujets. — Prix : 5 fr.

RANUNCULÆFLORUM; fl. en forme de renoncule, extra pleine, sans le moindre centre, les fleurs ont 5 cent. de diamètre, bombées, globuleuses, les pétales très-serrés sont bien imbriqués et un peu renversés, sa couleur est un très-beau bleu de cobalt pur; le centre des pétales est éclairé de blanc.

Cette plante a un beau port, une taille moyenne, des fleurs totalement pleines d'une forme admirable et bien disposées sur les rameaux, elle réunit toutes les qualités nécessaires pour être placée au premier rang de tous les Delphiniums connus. Le dessin, quoique beau, qui accompagne quelques prix-courants ne donne qu'une faible idée de la beauté de cette plante.

Livrable en bon sujets. — Prix : la pièce, 6 fr. — 3 plantes, 12 fr.

---

delphiniums, some ten of which had fully double florets and which had sky-blue, mid-blue, violet-blue, and indigo in their colour range. The eldest of the three generations of Lemoine maintained a deep interest in the delphinium for some seventy years until his death in 1911, his wife likewise. This firm bred delphiniums throughout that period and their son Émile, who died in 1942, carried on the work. Their last eighteen new intro-ductions were effected as late as the period 1919–33.

In England, James Kelway, who had founded a nursery at Langport in Somerset, imported the best plants from France and began breeding delphiniums on a big scale. Between them these two firms alone introduced no less than 1,091 distinct plants – quite apart from seed and seedlings distributed – in the period from 1878 to 1918. They popularized the plant to such an extent that they inspired seventy-four other breeders to follow suit, who in the same period produced a further 730 plants between them. Thus the gardening public was satiated with delphiniums – 1,821 of them in the short space of forty years.

Kelway's share of this was 728 varieties and they received a hundred Awards of Merit in all. As will be seen, the life of a new variety at that time was inconsiderable; varieties were rapidly displaced. Of all the plants the two breeders raised two stood out head and shoulders above their fellows – Lemoine's 'Statuaire Rude' and Kelway's 'King of Delphiniums'. By modern standards both had their faults of course, but 'Statuaire Rude' provided 3-in. florets of pure heliotrope, and 'King of Delphiniums', which had 2-in. plum-coloured florets with tips of gentian on the outer petals and a white eye, was very striking. Both were of semi-double formation. The French plant, as will be seen later, had an immense effect on breeding, and the Langport plant, though introduced in 1893 was still good enough for an Award of Merit after trial thirty-two years later.

New plants were introduced at such a pace that they were often here today and gone tomorrow. The novelty value was great and enthusiasm infectious, but constitution and perenniality left a great deal to be desired. Even a famous plant like 'Statuaire Rude' was suspect inasmuch as it had a very coarse and fleshy stem and was difficult to keep through the winter. Another factor which led to increased mortality was that the only generally known means of propagation was by division – a method which can so easily be a failure. In retrospect it can now be seen that far too much breeding was haphazard and promiscuous. Crosses were made, of course, but most of the new varieties came from choosing the best seedlings from natural seed. Little if anything was done at the time to stabilize desirable perennial qualities for future generations of plants. Nevertheless several very fine plants emerged from these sowings and such a one was 'Rev. E. Lascelles'. This plant was of a bright royal blue with a conspicuous white 'bee' or 'eye'. It was semi-double in form and very attractive indeed. Its quality may well be judged by the fact that, though a chance seedling sown about 1895, and one of a box of seedlings given to a Bath nurseryman, by name A. A. Walters, and raised by him, it gained an Award of Merit as a flower for exhibition in 1907 and an award after trial in 1925. When I add that it is still listed by Roger of Pickering, Yorks., in 1959, it will readily be seen that this was a momentous introduction.

The donor of the box of seedlings was the late Charles F. Langdon of Bath, who first became interested in delphiniums about 1890. I am told that right from the beginning Mr Langdon

6. 'Julia Langdon' is bright amethyst and a very good 'doer'

had a clear picture of his ideal delphinium. He insisted that it should be perennial with a really strong constitution and thus founded a worthy tradition which is certainly carried on at Bath to this day, seventy years later. But in purchasing the initial stocks from Lemoine and Kelway to form the Bath collection and breeding stud it soon became clear that two adverse qualities had been inherited – a proneness to mildew and a predominance of fat and fleshy stems such as 'Statuaire Rude' which caused heavy winter losses by reason of water stagnating in the cut-down stumps and setting up rot in the stool. Both these grave faults – and 'Rev. E. Lascelles' was a sufferer from mildew – proved very dominant in breeding and have taken the best part of forty years to control. It is given to few to have the strength of mind to destroy ruthlessly an apparently beautiful seedling just because it is a bad mildew subject or is particularly susceptible to wet winters. But at Bath it has been done for many years and it is only by such rigid selection that weakness can be eliminated. By now, more than a hundred years since the first hybrids were offered, breeders realize that the naming of a plant in a highly competitive field carries with it a responsibility. Institutions like The Royal Horticultural Society's Wisley Trials and the judgements passed on new varieties by the Joint Delphinium Committee, of which more later, help greatly in upholding the necessary high standard, though being by no means infallible.

By 1907 the fruits of Blackmore and Langdon's breeding began to be offered to the public. They already had a first-class collection of the best that Lemoine and Kelway could offer; to it they added such well-known varieties as 'Harry Smetham' and 'Robert Cox' of their own raising, but the outstanding event, and one that was to have a very big bearing on their line-breeding and on breeding elsewhere in England and in U.S.A. was the raising in 1910 of the two varieties 'Sir Douglas Haig' and 'Millicent Blackmore'. These two plants were named and exhibited after the war and both were at once given Awards of Merit as exhibition flowers and, later, after trial at Wisley. Both were semi-double, with florets about $2\frac{1}{2}$ ins. across, and with large spikes of good width. 'Millicent Blackmore' especially was wide at the base, and pale rosy mauve in effect, with sky-blue tips to the back petals and a large dark brown eye. 'Sir Douglas Haig' was a good purple on the front or inner petals with gentian tips to the back or outer petals.

These two plants achieved instant approval and popularity and marked a milestone in delphinium breeding. Each had 'Statuaire Rude' as one parent; despite the latter's faults opinion at Bath today still is that it had a greater influence on the evolution of the modern delphinium than any other variety ever raised. 'Statuaire Rude' was imported by Blackmore and Langdon in 1906, and also went to America. Later, cuttings and seed of both the new plants went to various growers in the U.S.A. 'Millicent Blackmore' gave very good seedlings from self-fertilized seed, and with 'Sir Douglas Haig' became the foundation breeding stock of the so-called Wrexham Hollyhock delphiniums, bred by Watkin Samuel between the wars, as well as being used by Hewitt's of Stratford-on-Avon to produce some of their best varieties during the same period.

At Bath breeding went on with less and less reliance on the seedling from self-fertilized seed. As knowledge and records were built up so the line breeding was intensified, the aim being vigorous and perennial constitution, coupled with hard stems and freedom from mildew. As to colour, 'Statuaire Rude' was heliotrope, and the mauves have thus always had a lead in the matter of size. From whatever source they come the mauves invariably have larger florets and spikes than the self blues even to the present day; at Bath that is attributed to the influence of 'Statuaire Rude'. Some thirty new varieties were registered from Bath before 1918, between the wars a further 152 in a twenty-year stretch and another hundred have been introduced from 1940 to 1959. A high percentage of notable plants, which have had useful commercial lives varying between ten and thirty years are included in those figures and the cumulative effect of proper records of some fifty years of purposeful line-breeding, through three generations of the Langdon family, began achieving its natural reward. After 1919 there followed such plants as sky-blue and single 'Mrs Townley Parker' (1923), deep amethyst 'The Shah' (1924), bright cornflower-blue 'Mrs Paul Nelke' (1927), double 'Mrs Foster Cunliffe' (1927), double 'Lady Eleanor' (1930),

7. A corner of the author's garden, showing, left to right, groups of a Blackmore and Langdon seedling, 'Ivy Ridgwell' and 'Dame Fortune'

ultramarine 'Blue Gown' (1931), light sky-blue 'Lady Emsley Carr' (1931), purple and deep blue 'Sir Neville Pearson' (1932), cornflower-blue 'A. J. Moir' (1933), plum-purple and gentian 'W. B. Cranfield' (1934), silvery mauve 'Tessa' (1936), sky-blue and rose 'Crystal' (1939), silvery mauve 'Bridesmaid' (1940), and lobelia-blue 'Valentia' (1940), most of which are still in cultivation, all being semi-double in form except where stated. To produce fifteen such notable plants out of a total of 152 introductions between the wars was a tremendous achievement.

Meanwhile, what of the other breeders? Certainly the delphinium was even more popular between the wars than it was prior to 1914. The drive for new varieties amounted to little short of a craze and I find that, in addition to the 152 from Bath already referred to, an amazing total of 107 breeders introduced the formidable number of 1,223 new plants in the twenty years from 1919 to 1939. There were undoubtedly a few really good plants amongst these but the percentage of real success was very small indeed and the breeders concerned have left no real mark on the family of plants. Most of the 1,223 plants had short-lived popularity because they simply were not up to standard.

One of the early exceptions to this condemnation was C. Ferguson, an amateur living at Weybridge in Surrey. He and his gardener, F. W. Smith, had the essential thoroughness in their make-up and a rigid idea of quality and vigour in their plants. As a result, in a very short space of time between 1912 and 1920, he produced four really outstanding plants in rosy lavender; 'Lavanda' (1912), light mauve and sky-blue 'Marjorie Ferguson' (1920), sky-blue with rosy flush 'Nora Ferguson' (1916), and pure gentian and white eye 'F. W. Smith' (1919). All were semi-double long-lasting garden plants of really desirable quality. All gained awards and were quickly taken up by the trade. Mr Ferguson's seed was distributed also, and three of the named varieties mentioned are still offered by several nurserymen forty years after introduction. It should be mentioned that Blackmore and Langdon, who had by 1920 begun to emerge as the leading breeders, considered all these plants worth adding to their collection. They still offered 'F. W. Smith' up to 1942 – a great tribute to its merit.

It is of course a matter of history that the late Frank Bishop began breeding about 1930, but the results of his work did not really become apparent until after the Second World War when he turned professional with Bakers of Codsall. His delphiniums have rightly become famous as the Bishop Strain and the Commonwealth Strain and his principal plants of note are still with us. They are dealt with fully in the second part of this chapter and in Chapter 13. At this point it should be recorded that Frank Bishop owed a great deal to the late Charles F. Langdon who afforded him practical help when he began breeding, and facilities to visit the Bath nursery, as well as visiting him at Windsor and advising on propagation, feeding, etc. At that time true blue semi-double delphiniums of real quality could be numbered on the fingers of one hand and Frank Bishop's purpose was to supply a real want by breeding blues up to the quality of the mauves – a worthy subject for line-breeding, if ever there was one. He duly recorded that his breeding stud included 'Mrs Paul Nelke', 'A. J. Moir', and 'Blue Gown' as well as three or four others from Blackmore

8. The late Frank Bishop of Codsall
   (Copyright *Express and Star*, Wolverhampton)

and Langdon, and the 1929 sky-blue semi-double 'Hunsdon Dell' bred by that great lover of the delphinium, T. Bones of Cheshunt.

With this stud as a foundation Frank Bishop began breeding for true and intense blue. There were three other developments between the wars which must not go unrecorded – three new strains in fact. Two of these strains, those of Karl Foerster in Germany and Watkin Samuel of Wrexham, have practically disappeared. The third, however, that of Frank Reinelt in California, was an entirely new conception as it was a seed strain, pure and simple, and has had a big bearing on world cultivation of the plant, as will be seen.

Today, little is known of Karl Foerster's work at Bornheim because it is in Eastern Germany and communication is very unsatisfactory. His 1959–60 list offers thirty-two delphiniums, of which thirty are of his own raising, and which seem to be *elatum* types. This is in strong contrast to his pre-war work of which, of course, more is known.

In fact, between 1921 and 1937 he registered no less than seventy new introductions. It would not be right to think of these in terms of the *elatum* hybrids we have been discussing, for none of them was semi-double, none was large-flowered, and purity of blue coupled with complete perenniality was his sole criterion. To achieve this end he spurned the garden hybrids as breeding material and concentrated solely on the wild plants, *D. elatum*, *D. grandiflorum* and the *belladonna* delphiniums which we shall discuss in Chapter 9. The colouring of his plants became marvellously pure, in all shades of blue through turquoise and peacock to deepest indigo, the stems were slim and tough and the constitution was impeccable. The florets themselves were, however, small and invariably single-petalled; thus they were not sufficiently far removed to displace the *belladonnas*, and had not the massive impressiveness to fill the need for blue in the *elatum* hybrids. It is a fact, of course, that these hybrids have themselves come from the wild *D. elatum*, so Karl Foerster was using the same material as Victor Lemoine.

All hybrids of all genera stem from the wild plant by man's manipulation. In many cases, and notably with the rhododendron, the continued use of selected forms of species which have for

26

centuries come true from seed, secure in their mountain valleys from man's meddling hands, has been beneficial, nay essential, in fixing the desired qualities in the progeny. Much the same is sometimes said of other plant families; in the case of the delphinium any effect the wild plants exerted is almost a thing of the past. Once used, as they had to be, they were rapidly cast aside. Who is to say that Karl Foerster was wrong in using them as he did?

To help the reader to understand the point about single flowers and semi-double flowers, I should mention that single-flowered types all cast off their petals in favour of seed-production much more quickly than semi-doubles do–a delphinium anomaly, in fact.

We have already seen how the Wrexham collection started with two notable plants from Bath, both progeny of 'Statuaire Rude'. From this beginning of two semi-double *elatum* varieties about 1920, Watkin Samuel turned out some seventy varieties, sixty between the wars and ten subsequently. Despite being offered to Blackmore and Langdon and refused, these plants had a great vogue both in England and in the U.S.A., where seed changed hands at higher and higher prices. Yet it is very doubtful indeed if they contributed anything permanent to the modern delphinium. Certainly, history supports Allan Langdon's judgement.

Looking back at them from a distance, with the excitement they created quite died down, I would say myself that there were among them four plants which showed a desirable type of progress, two pre-war and two post-war, yet each had a major fault from a breeding point of view:

'Blue Beauty' (1935) – a perfect blue of good constitution which was successfully taken up by the trade in general, gaining awards after trial and as an exhibition flower. The florets were single, however, and it has had to give precedence to improved forms, though still obtainable.

'Cambria' (1921) – a rosy lavender of semi-double and close formation with a heavy spike. It gained both awards but had very fleshy stems which were always among the first to break in bad weather.

'Watkin Samuel' (1946) – one of the purest deep sky-blue semi-doubles ever seen. An outstandingly beautiful plant to look at when well grown and one which the introducers, Bakers of Codsall, managed to show superbly for several years. Everyone, both trade and amateur, wanted it but none could keep it, for it proved to have a poor constitution.

'Boningale Glory' (1947) – this pretty and more than semi-double mixture of pale mauve and blue is a good 'doer' and is still leading a useful life. It grows 7 ft to 8 ft high, however, which is a disadvantage.

The singleness of the petals was a characteristic of many of the Wrexhams. They were normally too tall and much subject to damage. When seen against the background of a hundred years of breeding they have in fact contributed little to the advancement of the delphinium and were in several respects retrograde, thus proving once again that line-breeding plus ruthless selection and the highest standards is essential to lasting progress. Those who wish to understand more fully the importance of line-breeding and the dangers of promiscuity are referred to Chapters 4 and 6 on Seedling Raising and Breeding for the Amateur respectively.

At about the same time as the Wrexhams were at the height of their popularity the Bath strain was at a crucial point where in 1936 alone no less than 136 controlled crosses had been made amongst plants which were in many cases the descendants of the same initial stock as that used by Watkin Samuel. The results of these crosses, which have stood the test of time, and of all subsequent crosses in a line-breeding scheme, have been offered annually in increasing quality, performance, and range. Progress, in terms of breeding, which is a slow business, is spectacular, and this comes from a continual process of building up knowledge of the plants, generation after generation. As you will see, after the war and a mere thirty years, the same may be said of Frank Bishop, who proceeded on much the same lines but with a different initial objective.

Of course the sole object of the main breeders, Victor Lemoine, Kelways, Blackmore and Langdon, Frank Bishop, and others was to select and name the best seedlings. Rather than break in at this point with definitions I have assumed that it is common knowledge that in the case of the delphinium an original seedling

9. Frank Reinelt at work at Capitola, within sight of the Pacific Ocean

of high quality is a single plant and that it cannot be multiplied by raising more seedlings from its seed. Increase of a plant has to be effected by lifting the plant, dividing it up, or taking cuttings. As all seedlings are different and life is competitive, it is natural to give the accolade to the best alone. Seed and seedlings, of untested calibre, are sold annually in vast quantities, it is true, and with fine results, but for those who want the tried and tested article the named plant is the thing, and it is as well to realize that there are years of work behind that plant before the public can buy it.

Now in California, U.S.A., where the remaining breeder of current and front-rank importance began his task, the original plan was exactly the same but the climate provided eleven months of growing conditions and only one month of rest. If a breeder felt urged to breed delphiniums he therefore had to re-orientate his ideas around this central factor that perennials were strictly barred because they would have no dormancy in which to gather strength for next season's performance. Such a man was Frank Reinelt. A Czech by birth, he left his post as Head Gardener to Queen Marie of Rumania in 1925 to take a post in California. Till then his only knowledge of delphiniums was of a few of the species, but on arrival he found well-grown plants from British seed in many of the gardens and so formed an ambition to breed the genus. A start was made with seed from the Blackmore and Langdon Strain, the Wrexham Strain, and seed from two American amateurs who worked on the delphinium all their lives – Major F. Vanderbilt and Dr Leon Leonian. Frank Reinelt quickly discovered that to grow his plants as perennials was impossible on the Pacific seaboard. It is quite true that, as in most countries the world over, there are localities where conditions can be found closely resembling those in which *D. elatum* itself grows and it is always possible to treat the plants as perennials successfully in such sites. The requisite conditions are provided in mountain valleys where there is warmth in the growing season and where an unremitting and hard winter blankets the plants with snow and frost. Even in Great Britain we rarely have such conditions and in those frequent winters when losses of plants are suffered it is normally because a false spring or spell of mild weather occurs in January or February to coax up the shoots prematurely, only to be harshly treated by returning frost, cold wind, snow, and hail. In Siberia, the Swiss Alps, Afghanistan, in the mountains of East Africa, Abyssinia, and Tibet wild plants thrive for the reason stated.

And so, where our own conditions in Great Britain usually leave a lot to be desired, those in California, where plants frequently grow right throughout the whole twelve months, made it quite impossible to treat the delphinium as a perennial. The weather conditions over the whole of U.S.A. were with few exceptions similar, thus forcing the breeder to concentrate on growing for seed. The sun was always there, and the only other requirement was water, which can be supplied by irrigation or by overhead spray lines and under these conditions seed sown in October/November flowers splendidly in April, further shoots come up to be thinned to flower in late June and July, and a third crop can normally be expected in September.

Other climates mean other pests too, and in California's genial sunshine the host weeds remain nice and green the year round so that the leaf-hopper which transmits a virus called green-flower virus has to be dealt with, and the clearing of the ground every autumn for a new planting of seedlings is a helpful step.

10. Part of the plantation at Capitola in 1959, showing the Giant
Pacific seedlings

To satisfy the American market an annual quantity of seed
approaching 300 lb. is needed, and most of it has always been
grown in California because the calm and sunny conditions are
perfect for seed crops. As there are about 10,000 seeds to the
ounce the size of the problem can be appreciated. To that end,
Frank Reinelt began work and for a few years he marketed his
Giant Pacific seed strain as a mixture, just as all the other strains
were distributed, until he conceived the idea of separating the
seed into colours so that it could be marketed to flower true to
colour. This was an entirely new conception and after many
years of breeding it proved very successful and popular. Various
wild plants and several other breeders played an important part
in the project. Vanderbilt's *D. scopulorum* hybrids gave thin hard
cane-like stems with great resistance to mildew, Leonian's
hybrids gave improved selfs in the light mauve and amethyst
colour range, and the Hoodacre strain of white delphiniums –
founded on a single albino from British seed – gave the pure white
material on which to work. The mountains of Western America
hold large stands of a scarlet wilding, *D. cardinale*, and although
this plant is a diploid with only sixteen chromosomes, doubling
to thirty-two occurs naturally at times and a drug called colchicine
is sometimes successful in achieving the same result artificially.

31

Thus this species was brought into use in the hope of producing scarlet hybrids, but this aim had to be discarded because small single-petalled flowers of a violet shade predominated.

This experiment was not entirely abortive however. To this day among Giant Pacific seedlings attractive blush-coloured plants often arise, and the blue shades offered have a brilliance all their own. Both factors are attributed to the *D. cardinale* blood, which worked satisfactorily in a biennial seed strain, but which in more perennial conditions could have evinced weakness of constitution.

How did Reinelt proceed in order to produce seed which would flower ninety per cent white? Roughly, he took the two best-formed white plants and crossed them. From the resultant seedlings he again selected the two best white and crossed them, all other plants being scrapped, and in this way a true seed series was arrived at which could be relied upon. But he soon found that, if he consistently raised plants from hand-crossed seed only year after year, when plants were left to fertilize themselves they tended to lose the faculty of setting the seed and became sterile. And on the other hand he also found that in a test of plants left to self-fertilize for several years, without any selection and crossing of the best, the turn for the worse in quality was very noticeable. In short the method he has perfected, after establishing a colour series as desired above, is to self-fertilize for one year or possibly two in order to preserve the faculty for seed-setting, then to select and hand-cross the best plants in order to preserve colour, quality, and formation – ringing the changes in other words. I shall have more to say on this subject in later chapters in which I hope to make these rather complex matters clearly intelligible.

Meanwhile Giant Pacific seed can now be obtained the world over, not only in mixture but also in twelve quite distinct colour series, each of which is a clear self colour. For fifteen years before and during the last war the raiser went on experimenting and improving on his very definite plan and it is well known that his seed, founded very largely on British seed strains in the first instance, has come back to Great Britain in large quantities, not only for garden adornment but for use in breeding.

On the subject of the man himself – always an interesting

factor – I have been privileged to read all he has written on his favourite subject, and in addition I have had quite a series of interesting and illuminating letters from him. In U.S.A. he has achieved the highest honours, and his seed series are famous all over the world; for many years, in many countries with climates similar to the coastal plain of California, they have been the sole means of giving the enjoyment of modern delphiniums in the full colour range to many thousands of keen gardeners. I would say of Frank Reinelt that he is nothing if not thorough, an adaptable breeder with sustained enthusiasm and energy, and the very highest standards. In their different spheres and eras, and with their widely differing purposes, Charles F. Langdon and he really shared the greatest possible love for their subject plant. I feel sure that had they changed places the results might well have been the same.

Many other breeders have worked on the delphinium and had their moderate successes, but so far as I know none of them has had a definite sustained plan of line-breeding to an objective. Their small contribution to the general well-being has been made principally by having their plants incorporated into the line-breeders' collections for experimentation. The only exception to this rule is Edward Steichen of Connecticut, an amateur, whose fifty years of intensive breeding has been genetically sound, but who is such a perfectionist that it is only very recently that he has agreed to distribute his results, further reference to which is made in Chapter 9.

To the best of my ability I have just given you a general picture of the developments in breeding hybrids from about 1840 to 1940. It should be clear that the whole family of hybrids everywhere is closely inter-related, that very few wild delphiniums have played any part at all, that from 1880 to 1940 there were far too many 'breeders' hastily selecting far too many plants, and that, beginning with Blackmore and Langdon about 1910 and continuing with Frank Reinelt and Frank Bishop in 1925 and 1930 respectively, the merits of line-breeding and ruthless selection have been amply demonstrated. Had this sanity not returned to the scene it is certain that the delphinium would never have reached the pinnacle it is on today. Raisers and public alike were far too prone to accept plants at their face value when in bloom, and that can be cruelly deceptive.

As to the plants themselves, looking back at the inter-war period, far too many were single-flowered, there were too many with gross stems and disproportionately small flowers, mildew was rife, winter losses were excessive, the general height of the plants was too great, the pure blue colour was very poorly represented, and the general colour range in Great Britain was restricted to a very few first-class blues, many light and medium amethysts and mauves, plus mixtures. It now remains to see, therefore, how the line-breeding by Blackmore and Langdon, Frank Reinelt, and Frank Bishop has completely changed this picture in the post-war period.

The Present

We have already seen that the late Frank Bishop of Windsor and Codsall was attracted to the delphinium about 1930 by the disparity of numbers and quality which he noted between the mauves and the blues then available. There are of course limits beyond which no breeder may go with impunity and there is the greatest possible virtue in standing by a proved and methodical breeding plan. In the case of Blackmore and Langdon their policy was first and foremost to produce garden plants of real stamina, healthy, mildew-free, shapely, well-proportioned, and of the greatest possible longevity. No one, least of all Charles F. Langdon, his son Allan, or his grandson Brian, disregards the value of colour.

Indeed, Allan Langdon is recorded as saying in a lecture at Beckenham as long ago as 1935:

Imagine for a second the scope for the hybridist in the production of true blue varieties. We have as yet only the nucleus. The true blue semi-doubles can be numbered on one hand, and some of these will only give of their best in special soils. I am often being reminded that we growers are going away from the true blues; I reply that it is not a case of going away from them, as we have never had them, only in the single types, and while these have had their uses, I think their days are numbered, and that singles will eventually almost disappear from cultivation as a propagated plant.

At Bath, therefore, colour – and blue in particular – was fully

11. Allan Langdon among the delphiniums at Bath

appreciated but it had to come through natural breaks out of a plan based on real perenniality and quality. Therefore colour, in itself, was a secondary consideration. And at the time in question the weight of opinion at Bath was that directed hybridization on the lines indicated had reached the threshold only, that breaks in various desirable directions could be confidently expected, and at an increased tempo. I shall refer again to this confident prediction a little later.

Meanwhile, as Allan Langdon was speaking at Beckenham, Frank Bishop was working in his spare time at Windsor on the blue stocks he had acquired in an endeavour to produce blue delphiniums as good as the mauve. His breeding plan, though begun with hardy stocks, put colour as his primary objective, and it was certainly designed to fill a real gap in the delphinium ranks. At that time the top-class plant 'Blue Gown', introduced from Bath in 1931 from a seedling raised in 1925 (and still offered by some nurserymen in 1960!), and 'F. W. Smith', raised by C. Ferguson as long ago as 1914 and still obtainable, were still the two best blue delphiniums, a fact which speaks for itself as both were relatively small in the flower. There were also such varieties as 'A. J. Moir', 'Hunsdon Dell', and 'Lady Emsley Carr', all three of which were worthy introductions, but as garden plants none of the three had the stamina really necessary.

35

With this material at hand Bishop had produced a small collection of improved blues by the outbreak of the Second World War and they were duly introduced through Bakers of Codsall, whom he joined in 1945. At this stage the plants were merely a small improvement on existing British blues and it was not until the impact of the Giant Pacific 'Blue Jay' seed, which he had imported in 1940, was fully felt that the breeder began to attain the vivid blue colour and size of floret which he had always had in the forefront of his mind. Of the first set of semi-doubles made available from the seedlings out of the 'Blue Jay' crosses, purest gentian 'Jerry Wells', silvery blue 'Harvest Moon', cornflower-blue 'Anne Page', Reckitt's blue 'Agnes Brooks' with its gay blue and white striped eye, and gentian 'Mrs Frank Bishop' were the best. In size of floret and brightness of blue in all its shades they certainly represented a very big advance. One of the finest to look at in colour and formation was 'Jerry Wells', large-flowered as were all the others. But it deteriorated rapidly and had a short life as a plant. 'Anne Page' had the best constitution and is still going strong after fourteen years in commerce but it is a comparatively dull blue compared with the others. Three of these are still in commerce and are very attractive indeed although they have that little bit lacking in formation and constitution which prevented them reaching the top rank. It was inevitable that, in using 'Blue Jay' and its size of florets and brilliance of colour, the breeder should have to accept with it its inherent weaknesses when grown in England as a perennial instead of as a biennial in U.S.A. He felt compelled to take a risk which the Bath breeding plan would have ruled out of court and in doing so he certainly lost ground in point of constitution and perenniality. Results since 1945–7 seem, however, to have justified his risk because the brilliant blue has been retained and constitution improved, evidenced by such varieties as sky-blue 'Caprice' and 'Skylark', gentian 'Robin Hood', darker blue 'Jack Tar', cornflower 'Fidelity', silvery blue 'Nora O'Fallon', and bright mid-blue and white eye 'Sparkling Eyes'. Undoubtedly these, and others, are first-class plants by any standards.

But the infusion of American blood from a strain with a very wide colour range undoubtedly affected the Bishop strain in

12. (*left*) 'Robin Hood', newest and one of the best of the violet and
    gentian blues from the Bishop strain. Fine and graceful tapering
    spikes, on slim stems and well supplied with laterals to carry on
    the display

13. (*right*) Famous 'Swanlake', a fine garden plant though a trifle
    narrow at the base

other ways also. Whilst maintaining his love of the popular blue,
the breeder found he was getting breaks in other directions, such
as white, heliotrope, and Parma-violet. These were followed up
and have resulted in a series of fine perennials as exemplified by
off-white 'Swanlake' with its black eye, heliotrope 'Cinderella'
with her perfect habit, snow-white 'Purity', and violet 'Minstrel
Boy'. Whilst Frank Bishop had built up such a reputation for
bright blue that the phrase 'a real Bishop Blue' had been
commonly accepted and used by breeders and amateurs alike, the

14. The 4-in. florets of that magnificent Commonwealth plant, 'Canada', in shades of pale heliotrope and light blue

Codsall collection began to swell into as wide a colour range as the Giant Pacific. To my mind it has come to represent the British version of what Frank Reinelt dreamed of doing when he first set out but found impossible – a perennial version of the Giant Pacific colour range with an underlying note of British constitution and perenniality about it.

Development at Codsall was not to stop at this, however. Back in 1948 a seedling appeared which had qualities which singled it out from all its fellows. Florets were 4 ins. across, of perfect formation, the foliage was large above the ordinary and completely immune to mildew, and the plant was vigorous. It took four more years of line-breeding to obtain the right results but it was done, and thus was laid the foundation of the strain known as Commonwealth, all the plants of which are distinguished for their outsized florets, spikes, and foliage, together with very great mildew resistance. They may be typified by heliotrope 'Great Britain', an A.M. plant, pale heliotrope and sky-blue 'Canada', and palest heliotrope 'Ceylon'. All are plants of perfect proportions, and have elegant tapering stems, with the width of spike fully in keeping with the remarkable foliage.

The breeder has stated clearly that no Giant Pacific blood was brought into the breeding plan for this strain, though the colours point that way unmistakably. Despite the evident throwback to a strain which was bred as biennial these plants certainly tend to prove that when treated as perennials in British conditions wise selections are fully capable of standing up to any test. 'Great Britain' has performed well up to standard in the R.H.S. Trials at Wisley and also at Bath where Blackmore and Langdon added it to their collection.

With the advent of the Commonwealth strain, the Codsall collections, and indeed the seed strain, do not offer a marked predominance of blue any longer. The pendulum has swung the other way, in fact. When seed of the Bishop strain was first offered in 1947 the resultant seedlings were predominantly and impressively blue. That predominance now seems to have ceased, but with the addition of heliotrope, violets, whites, and various pastel shades to the named collection, the seed mixture affords an astonishing variety of great quality. Such self-fertilized seed has given many very fine plants which have received Awards of Merit, such as sky-blue 'Daily Express', rich blue 'Evening Standard', and pure white 'Sunday Express'. All of these are in commerce and the first-named has a wide distribution. All three help to prove the ultimate real value of the work which the breeder did in his attempt to ally Californian purity and brightness of colour to British perenniality.

Frank Bishop indeed helped very considerably to alter the pre-war picture of a delphinium. His varieties, of which more detail will be found in later chapters and of which there are several illustrations, all conform to the improved standards everyone welcomes. All are semi-double, all have elegant and graceful stems, with florets and spikes fully in proportion with foliage and height of plant, and with very few exceptions the heights are greatly reduced, with many from 4 ft to 5 ft only. Resistance to mildew is generally excellent and the collections show good judgement in selection and a high standard of rogueing – in all, the finest possible memorial to a great plant-lover and a competitive factor of real value.

A point not yet mentioned is the length of the flowering season. Before the war there were plenty of signs that this was receiving attention at Bath, especially in production of later flowering plants. But one of the outstanding features of Frank Bishop's introductions is that many of the plants flower earlier than usual and thus tend to throw up a second time with success. This trait is of course notable with the Giant Pacific seed series as they have been bred specifically for early flowering from seed and repetitive display. The pre-war flowering season in any general collection in Great Britain, from the time the bottom florets opened until the latest of the laterals dropped, may be put at about six or seven weeks, whereas nowadays, with the judicious use of late-flowering varieties from Bath plus selected plantings of early Bishops and of Giant Pacific seedlings, this would be extended to nine or ten weeks, a big advance and one in keeping with general developments amongst other genera.

What of developments in California since the outbreak of the last war? Outside the U.S.A. very little was known about the Giant Pacific strain before that time but after the war seed began to be imported and distribution over the years has been pretty general among trade and amateur growers alike. Personal observation suggests that the seed met with a favourable response from gardeners who wanted cheap delphiniums. Undoubtedly the reason was that it always held the promise of an interesting and wide colour range and that it had been bred over so many years to flower quickly. This meant that the gardener got comparatively quick results in the shape of big spikes and the brightest of self colours. It should be noted here that only a small minority have enjoyed the separate colour series from seed ripened in California. Most of the experience in Great Britain is from seed harvested here and distributed as a mixture, and in a few instances where seed has been offered to colour from British-grown plants the results have not been as reliable as they should be, as the qualities and colours are lost through continued self-fertilization and the absence of control. The few who take the trouble to import the raiser's own seed can fully enjoy the advantages of his steady improvement in quality and can select their colours to suit their taste. In U.S.A., Canada, South America, Australia, New Zealand, and South Africa those who wish to grow delphiniums are as up-to-date as residents in California since the seed they buy is either this year's or last year's Californian harvest. This, plus relative cheapness, is the great advantage of a seed series or a seed mixture as opposed to the purchase of named plants; from a specialist source the plants will be reliable and their qualities known, but they are naturally more expensive.

Obviously the Giant Pacifics have their faults when grown in Great Britain or elsewhere as perennials. They are not bred as such and some of their colours, particularly pink and white, often give plants of poor constitution. Some of the blues too, due to the blood of *D. cardinale*, are not long-living and do not make the big and impressive clumps which British perennials usually do. Nevertheless anyone raising a stock would be very unlucky indeed not to find sufficient reward in plants that were truly perennial. All types are particularly early to flower; the strain is in fact essential to anyone who wants really early flowering with the practical certainty of a second display each season, and the

41

15. The Giant Pacific 'Lancelot' series in bloom in California. Note slim and tapering spikes and size of floret

flowering of the plants does not in fact clash at all with the British productions, many of which flower later. The cheapness of raising new plants, to colour and otherwise, to replace those lost is an undeniable attraction.

It is often said against Frank Reinelt's plants that in some sorts the spikes are too loosely built. While to the experts and the purists such points of argument are understandable, to the general public colour and colour alone is the biggest attraction of all. Good, clear, and bright colours, raised in a garden at a negligible price per plant constitute a powerful argument. Very few people breed plants, exhibit them competitively, or try to increase any particular plant by means of division or cuttings. In these respects the Giant Pacifics might fall short and then again, in some cases, they have proved satisfactory. What really matters is that they increase the length of the delphinium season, and, by their cheapness *vis-à-vis* plants, encourage thousands of gardeners to grow delphiniums who might otherwise be unable to do so.

The stems are particularly slim, graceful, and weather-resistant, the quality of the individual florets both in size and purity of colour is unquestioned, the general height is commendably short, and the whole strain is highly resistant to the disfiguring mildew.

Here are the separate colours available in seed form from California:

'Lancelot' – large rounded florets of clear heliotrope with creamy-white bees, forming particularly well-built spikes (see Fig. 15).

'Guinevere' – rosy lavender self with a white bee, large 3-in. florets on long spikes.

'Cameliard' – a bi-colour with deep lavender inner petals and gentian blue on the frilly edge of the outers, large creamy-white bee. Florets of good size, evenly placed.

'King Arthur' – a rich plum-purple self, very good petal texture, large contrasting white bee. The stems are bronze and particularly slim and hard.

'Black Knight' – a very deep purple indeed without a touch of any other colour. The bees are black and the stems elegantly slender and whippy.

16. A Giant Pacific 'Summer Skies' seedling flowering in perfect form in Surrey – light blue with a creamy-yellow eye, plant four years old

'Astolat' – shades of pink, varying from palest blush up to deep raspberry rose, with the bees mostly fawn and black. The pink colours unfortunately are apt to bleach quickly in hot sunshine.

'Summer Skies' – light sky-blue with white bees, florets beautifully rounded (see Fig. 16).

'Blue Bird' – rich and pure mid-blue, a very bright colour, with a flat white bee.

'Blue Jay' – a very intense dark blue, with a black eye. (This is the plant used by Frank Bishop in his early breeding of blue perennials.)

'Galahad' – purest possible white of fine texture, large florets, white eye.

'Percival' – equally pure white, but with a jet black eye (see Fig. 79, page 201).

Round Table Mixture – a very fine seed mixture giving a high percentage of large florets, in all the colours above and many other mixtures of colour and variety of bee as well.

Figs. 9 and 10 give some idea of the pitch to which this great plantsman, Frank Reinelt, has brought his Seed Series. These pictures certainly amply demonstrate the quality and consistency of the seed series in the Californian climate. A great achievement in a short thirty years of breeding time.

Allan Langdon's confident prediction that singles would pass out of cultivation has, of course, already come true, for all the plants offered at Bath and at Codsall are semi-doubles or doubles, and the Giant Pacific seed strain gives no singles. At Bath, once the war was over, there began to be introduced a series of plants the foundation of which was laid in the last few years before the war began. Whereas the belief at Bath had always been that the sowing of promiscuous seed by the breeders generally had done the plant a disservice, the plants they now introduced have proved beyond any doubts that purposeful line-breeding is the only method by which the desired basic qualities of constitution, vigour, form, and resistance to mildew can be fixed in a breeding stud or collection.

The part played by Frank Bishop has already been outlined and appraised. From Bath about a hundred varieties have been introduced in the fifteen post-war years; the general standard has

45

been of the very highest and many notable advances have been made.

The biggest single achievement is perhaps still in the light mauves where a succession of fine plants has included 'Jennifer Langdon', 'Silver Moon', 'Ringdove', and 'Great Scot'. All are almost immune to mildew and have all the properties expected of a good perennial. Full descriptions of these and many others will be found in the Selected List of Varieties in Chapter 13.

Another important development has been the introduction of rich purple selfs. While this began modestly with the introduction of that well-habited but somewhat small-flowered variety 'Minerva', the plants which followed have all outdated it completely. It is sufficient to mention 'Tyrian', 'Turridu', 'Guy Langdon', 'Purple Triumph', and 'Sentinel', the last-named being the darkest and richest purple yet raised. In the all-important blue section, notable arrivals have included the famous 'Blue Rhapsody' which created a sensation at Royal Chelsea in 1948, sky-blue 'Charles F. Langdon' and 'May Docwra'; the purest light blue of all, 'Betty Hay'; and two exceptional 1959 introductions in vivid gentian 'Greville Stevens' with white eye and its counterpart, dark-eyed 'Mollie Buchanan'. These last two constitute a landmark in the Bath strain as regards the brightness and vividness of the blue and are certainly the equal in colour of anything yet bred in that respect. Whereas before the war it could rightly be said that delphiniums generally were hardly blue at all, the overall picture has since changed completely. The Bishop strain duly developed its pure blues and maintains them, but now shows its most dominating advance in Commonwealth mauves, heliotropes, and shades of violet, while at Bath the biggest single colour development is certainly the new series of striking blues, 'Greville Stevens', 'Mollie Buchanan', and 'Supermarine'. In both strains, for the first time, there is now direct and intense competition in both blue and light mauve; in white Codsall have a big lead and in purple selfs Bath has had a monopoly.

But the story does not end there. At Bath, a good perennial white has at long last been developed, 'Snow White' by name, and a series of short, semi-dwarf delphiniums in the mid-blue to dark blue shades has been developed, flowering at heights from 3 ft to 4 ft 6 ins. These include 'Blue Tit', 'Blue Jade', and 'Bebe'. The pedigree of 'Blue Jade' will be found in Chapter 6 on Breeding for the Amateur and affords much interesting study. At Codsall too, short-growing plants have appeared as natural mutations or 'breaks' and you have 'Blue Pearl', Parma-violet 'Minstrel Boy', sky-blue 'Caprice', and others. At present the difference is that at Bath six years of work have been put into these semi-dwarfs in a successful endeavour to breed them as a separate strain, and for some years a good nucleus of plants has existed. Interbreeding amongst them is successfully producing a dominant and highly desirable shortness of stature which is of the first importance to the twentieth-century gardener. Furthermore, at the time of writing, the seed from this separate strain is producing as much as eighty per cent semi-dwarfs and will probably be available to the gardening public as this book appears.

Pink delphiniums have also received attention at Bath and one, 'Deirdre', is in the R.H.S. Trials at Wisley and has a Highly Commended. But the fact is that, as with other pink named varieties, 'Deirdre' has not yet been listed because it lacks the vigour to propagate well enough.

To summarize the present, post-war, *vis-à-vis* the pre-war position – the coarse and fleshy stem has completely disappeared in favour of slimmer and harder stems; the single-petalled floret is entirely replaced by longer-lasting semi-double florets from 3 ins. to $4\frac{1}{2}$ ins. across; the height of plants has been very greatly reduced and a good number of plants flowering at 3 ft–4 ft 6 ins. is available; all three breeders have ruthlessly rogued plants prone to mildew and the strains are very resistant now; the colour range in Great Britain has been widened with the addition of many sound perennial whites, heliotropes, and Parma-violets; and, most important of all, the public now has a wide choice of the finest and purest blues imaginable, from light to dark, from early-flowering to late-flowering types. The last fifteen years' work has produced sounder and more spectacular progress than anything that went before. As one generation of plants has succeeded another, line-breeding has retained and almost fixed the good qualities and made them dominant. Still further improvement, on

17. Delphinium 'Guy Langdon' – a giant with 4 ft of bloom

the same plan, is a certainty for the future, as will be seen in Chapter 14.

Whilst Frank Reinelt and Frank Bishop have both done work of real value in their very different spheres, nothing in the whole history of our plant can ever be comparable with the work done at Bath. Line-breeding, controlled and recorded, was begun there by the far-sighted Charles F. Langdon in the early years of the century with imported stock plants. It has gone on for over fifty years and continuity for the future is assured. This is an un-rivalled and unchallengeable position which augurs well for the growing company of delphinium lovers.

2 · The delphinium in the garden

We have seen that the delphinium has never lacked attention from breeders of skill, actuated first and foremost by their love of the plant. This is a happy combination which always brings good plants into being. The basic colours of the delphinium are quiet, cool, and yet rich as well. They are colours which are not blatant, which satisfy and do not pall. They are always in the best gardening taste.

The plant itself has an upright or spicate habit and dominates in the border for that very reason, despite the fact that it is not scarlet or orange in colour. It dominates more subtly, in a truly noble and aristocratic manner, and owing to the way in which the florets are held on the stems it asserts its colour with equal effect from all angles. A well-grown plant, well sited, will always command attention from the eye of a flower lover. But it is a plant which benefits from its surroundings and from its companions, both by contrast and by blending.

The Setting

There are very few types of garden in which the delphinium will not look well. The lucky few who own, or are contemplating, walled gardens, whether of mellowed red brick, grey stone, slate, or flint-faced, can plant their delphiniums in the sure knowledge that they will fit in and appear thoroughly at home. With the red brick it is best to leave out the pale mauves, the amethyst, lavender, and heliotrope, and of course the pinks are anathema. The blues and purples and the violets and whites will suit admirably. With grey stone walls, or walling, or courtyards paved with stone, the mid-blues in particular provide a very lovely combination, and all colours are in keeping.

Such luxuries are for the few, however, and the problem of background and wind-break is for most of us one of the living screen or the wooden or wire fence. With the artificial background little can be done except to clothe it or hide it with green as much as possible. Trees, hedges, and shrubs, evergreen and

18. Close-up of 'Guy Langdon'

deciduous, offer the best solution. Herbaceous borders, whether they be island borders set in the middle of a lawn, single borders running down one side of a lawn, or twin borders, are always most effective in a living setting of green, grey, gold, or copper.

Admirable backgrounds for delphiniums are the glaucous conifers such as *Cupressus* 'Fletcheri' or 'Allumii', or at a distant view on a grander scale, groups of *Cedrus atlantica glauca* or Koster's spruce. The grey-green with blues and purples is a particularly rich and satisfying combination. In gold or yellow there is a wide choice, examples being variegated holly, *Elaeagnus*, such conifers as *Cupressus lawsoniana lutea*, *Taxus baccata aurea* (a golden seedling of the common yew), and the golden form of the Irish yew. There is also the golden privet and the blending of blue and gold, or purple and gold, is very striking. A planting I once saw and much admired was one of the bush form of *Prunus cerasifera atropurpurea* which, with its purple foliage closing in behind gentian delphiniums, was very rich and satisfying. Used as an informal hedge or as a small standard tree behind a formal live hedge it can be equally effective. In sites where formal hedging is employed such background trees as *Acer negundo variegata* in its green and silver or its green and gold forms, many of the lovely Japanese maples, or the purple-leaved form of *Malus purpurea*, the ornamental apple, can play an important part in enhancing the satisfaction and beauty of delphiniums and of the herbaceous borders in which they are a feature. There are of course many alternative shrubs, trees, and conifers which can be equally suitable.

With the formal living hedge as a background, or as part of a background completed by an outer screen of mixed conifers or trees, the choice becomes merely a matter of taste and patience. My personal preference is for yew, but holly, privet, hornbeam, beech, and many others can be made equally effective. All are hardy, and so long as the owner has the necessary patience they will suit. All formal hedges should be shaped with a good batter, that is, they should be considerably thicker at the base than at the top. This is a big factor in keeping the base healthy and well clothed with foliage and ensuring it has its fair share of sun and air. This in turn means that when the hedge is mature the delphiniums and other plants will still get the maximum of protection even at the base. One so often sees tall hedges in which all the new growth is at the top with the bottom bare and ugly and no longer draughtproof, not the best of protection for delphiniums.

The Companions

For those who study the flowering time of their named delphiniums and of the seedlings they selected from their seedling beds, there is no end to the happy garden incidents which can be worked out. The full modern delphinium range gives the gardener scope from the middle of the Russell lupin season to the time when the phlox are just showing colour – a good nine weeks anyway.

Thus, such delightful contrasts as are afforded by lupins such as corn-coloured 'Goldilocks' or 'Wheatsheaf', peach-pink and soft yellow 'Daydream', bright terracotta and yellow 'Louise', orange 'Festival', and pure pink 'Betty Astell' can be had with the delphiniums. The soft sky-blues and rich gentian blues of Giant Pacific 'Summer Skies' and 'Blue Bird', and of early-flowering named plants such as silvery blue 'Harvest Moon', sky-blue 'Caprice', gentian 'Evening Standard', brilliant sky-blue 'Artist', sky-blue 'Blue Dawn', richest blue 'Blue Rhapsody' will suit admirably. That lovely rich blue 'Cristella' is particularly early, the tall medium blue 'Charles F. Langdon' and the semi-dwarf royal blue and indigo 'Blue Tit' – all these and more besides are available to complement the lupins. All heights and all shades of blue are included; and if the plants detailed in Chapter 13 are studied carefully many lovely combinations can be worked out.

From mid-June we find possible such happy blendings as blue, purple, and violet shades of delphiniums with soft yellow anthemis and various varieties of helenium such as *H. pumilum* and 'Mme Canivet'; the gentian delphiniums also look particularly well growing from among the silvery foliaged *Artemisia gnaphalodes* or *ludoviciana*. Although also spicate in habit, *Verbascum vernale* with its yellow flowers, and *V. chaixii* with its silvered indumentum both have possibilities, and almost

52

any of the blue and purple delphiniums go with them admirably. A planting of *Achillea* 'Gold Plate' with rich purple or gentian delphiniums rising behind it can also be satisfactory, and in most cases the foliage of the earlier flowering paeonies can create pleasing contrasts both with the delphinium foliage as well as with the bloom. Thought should be given to the best use of foliage contrast for even the delphinium itself affords variety: some leaves are very finely divided and quite dainty, others are broader and bolder, some have a polished appearance and some are covered with fine soft hairs.

In colour of foliage and stem, the delphinium varies from the softest and tenderest spring green, through the darker greens, to bronze stems and leaves with touches of crimson on them.

White delphiniums are of most use in borders composed of white plants and foliage, or as a foil between groups of delphiniums of varying colours. They also look well in composite beds with gentian delphiniums, Madonna lilies, or *Lilium regale*. Another use for the whites is with herbaceous surrounds such as *Monarda didyma* 'Cambridge Scarlet', or Veronica 'Shirley Blue'.

The colour section of delphiniums which requires most thought, if the best is to be obtained from it, is that very strong section of silvery mauve, amethyst, lilac, and heliotrope shades. If the delicate pastel colourings are to be enjoyed to the full these plants are best used amongst the later-flowering perennials which at delphinium time will give foliage contrast and no possibility of colour-clash. An unorthodox but effective combination successfully tried by the author, using these delicately coloured delphiniums, is with autumn-sown sweet peas in the pale lavender and pale pink shades, grown in groups among the delphiniums on twiggy pea-sticks.

As for the pleasing combinations which can be achieved with the rose in all its forms, they are legion. A glimpse of well-grown delphiniums seen through a rose arch, a pergola of roses running along the back of a delphinium border, or pillar roses and delphiniums alternating at the back of a large herbaceous border – these can scarcely fail to look beautiful. I can still see in my mind's eye the end wall of a large barn built of mellowed grey stone, along the foot of which ran a herbaceous border. On the wall itself and covering it completely was that lovely and ever popular rose, golden buff 'Gloire de Dijon'. At the foot in full flower amongst a mass of silver *Artemisia gnaphalodes* were several plants of that fine gentian delphinium 'Sue Murrell' – the whole forming a most lovely picture.

Luxuries such as borders of delphiniums alone are for the specialist, for public parks, or for those few who have very large gardens; they need not be considered here. The delphinium is, however, no longer the prerogative of those who can afford large borders. Most gardeners are restricted by consideration of space or outlay or both. They no longer need to feel that the delphinium is not for them, for it has indeed become a plant of common appeal to all in these last ten years. I have in mind, particularly, the full selection of delphinium colours available now in heights from 3 ft 6 ins. to 5 ft. Such plants, and the fact that breeding of semi-dwarfs is actively proceeding at Bath both in named sorts and as a seed strain, surely mean that delphiniums are for all, however small the garden or the pocket.

As yet no mention has been made of the ever-expanding range of delphiniums which flower very late. These are particularly valuable to the herbaceous border at all altitudes and latitudes because they are the plants which ensure delphinium bloom at the peak time of the herbaceous border, even in some cases along with the *Phlox paniculata*. A full range of these late-flowering delphiniums is described in Chapter 13. As to the siting of the plants in the border, full use should be made of their height range to lift the eye-level of the border when in flower, to break up any suspicion of tiered regimentation, and to create restrained focal points here and there.

3 · Cultivation

The delphinium belongs to the plant order known as *Ranunculaceae* and numbers the anemone, the aquilegia, and love-in-a-mist among its fellows, as well as the ranunculus itself. It is a very hardy and long-living perennial plant which subsists on a fibrous root system as is shown in Fig. 20a. Its individual flower is referred to as a floret, of which anything from twenty-five to a hundred go to make up an individual spike. The florets are held to the main stem by means of pedicels, or little stems, which vary in length from 2 ins. to 15 ins. and are set at varying angles, thus causing columnar spikes (see Fig. 13) and pyramidal spikes (see Fig. 71).

Choosing Plants

As with all plants the delphinium ought really to be viewed in flower, when individual taste can come into play. If you are purchasing by post without viewing, it is essential to outline requirements and to deal with a firm noted for its delphiniums. And in the interests of health and longevity it is best to insist on plants which are one year old and no older, and which have been propagated from rooted cuttings and not from divisions (see Chapter 5).

The best method of all for plant and planting time is to purchase rooted cuttings, taking delivery from April to June. This is a plant somewhere between Fig. 38m and Fig. 38s in its stage of growth and is easily established. This method is only for the patient and thorough gardener, however, because no flowering can be permitted until September, all buds must be pinched out until mid-August, and the young plants must be well cultivated throughout the season if they are to build up properly.

You may also take one-year-old plants from September to November if your soil is at all on the light side or particularly well drained. These should be the spring cuttings grown on by the nurseryman for one season and no older, thus being young plants full of vigour, though quite small to look at. The exact time of delivery will depend upon suitable weather for lifting at the nursery, and on receipt the plants should be heeled in if the ground conditions are too dry or too soggy for permanent planting. This should be done when the soil is nicely and uniformly moist so that it crumbles well to receive the fibrous roots as widely separated as possible (see Figs. 19a, b, and c). The same season, September–November, is indicated for any transplanting you may have to do from one part of your garden to another (see Figs. 20a–f). The planting or transplanting of these plants, as opposed to the rooted cuttings, gives them a setback and the effect of this is greatly increased on light land if the work is undertaken in spring with flowering time a short three months ahead and it is for this reason that autumn planting is preferable. These soils are warmer than the heavy ones and, as I have proved, plentiful root growth will continue even up to the end of January. This gives these plants a real and extended hold upon the soil, which in turn enables them to take in enough nourishment that season to ensure a reasonable display and at the same time to remain in full vigour.

On medium and heavy soils these one-year-old plants should be left at the nursery until spring growth has commenced. The reason for this is that in cold and heavy land the young plants cannot make much root progress in September–January, and in a wet winter losses of such newly planted plants can be severe.

Preparation of Soil

The delphinium is a plant from which an impressive display is expected over the years. It therefore behoves us to give the plants a really good foundation before planting. The site or sites should be thoroughly dug two spits deep on all but the sandy soils where one spit is usually sufficient and more may well be dangerous. *Such digging should be done a good three months or more before planting is undertaken*, to permit the soil to settle, and planting should be really firm (see Figs. 20c, d, and e). Thus we have firm contact between soil and roots and uniform moistness, which can be retained for a long time by frequent and shallow surface hoeing. Planting in freshly dug ground is a grave error, because

19a. A new plant or division, prior to planting

19b. Note the pyramid of fine soil in the hole

19c. The new plant, with no ball of soil, fits the pyramid which facilitates the spreading out of the roots. The raking back of the soil, followed by firming as in Figs. 20d, e, and f ensures that the roots strike quickly

20a. Transplanting a matured seedling to a new position – note the ball of soil on the roots and the ample, bowl-shaped hole

20b. The same plant placed in its hole

20c. Three-quarters of the soil sifted back round the roots and packed in by hand

20d. Firming all round to ensure close contact between soil and root tips

20e. The appearance after firming

20f. The remaining soil raked back round the plant

59

sun and air have too free a passage and will rapidly dry out the roots of young plants.

Well-rotted humus should be plentifully incorporated during the digging process. Fresh humus causes heat when rotting and could damage the all-important root hairs which pick up all the nourishment. Leaf-mould, peat, spent hops, garden compost, and other such materials are splendid, as of course is farmyard strawy manure. On light land humus knits the soil, holds Nature's moisture, and retains liquid manures; on heavy land this same humus helps greatly also in breaking up the soil and preventing the fine soil granules from caking and becoming impenetrable to the roots.

For those who study their plants' needs, it is always good to incorporate coarse bone-meal (a single handful in each planting hole). It will be beneficial in promoting root growth and in hardening the stems. Lime in all its forms is unnecessary to the delphinium, which thrives in a slightly acid soil – a pH of 6·5 is usually ideal for the general run of herbaceous plants – and should only be used to sweeten soured soils. In such cases hydrated lime should be used on medium and heavy land, and finely ground chalk (carbonate of lime) on sandy soils at the rate of four oz. per sq. yd. All but the hungriest of soils normally contain some potash; on sandy soils it has to be provided and this need can be attended to quite simply by using pig or farmyard manure or composted seaweed, or by using sulphate of potash at the rate of ½ oz. per plant (see Chapter 12, p. 152). Lack of potash can result in serious loss of colour intensity.

The delphinium is not fussy about soil – heavy clay, light sand, or chalky soils, all can give fine spikes.

Surface Cultivation

In planted-up ground no deep forking of the soil round the plant should take place in the growing season. If enforced by neglect and excessive weed it may well damage the new roots which are near the surface from April to June. Better not to do it at all, and on light soils it undoubtedly helps to cause excessive drying out. Delphiniums make a heavy demand upon the moisture in the soil and constant shallow hoeing to conserve this, or a surface mulch to cut off evaporation, is by far the best method. Hoeing will also go a long way to discourage the delphinium's main enemy, the slug, which is later discussed.

Thinning

Thinning means the cutting out of some of the shoots, thus reducing the number of spikes to be formed. It is *not a special secret for the specialist or exhibitor* but an ordinary and sensible garden operation, to be completed by the time the shoots are 12 ins. tall (see Figs. 21a–f), and comparable to the pruning of roses and stopping and disbudding of dahlias and chrysanthemums.

In the season following planting or transplanting this thinning should be fairly drastic, not more than one or two spikes being allowed on new plants. If no thinning is undertaken the quality of the spike will be poor and disappointing, the height will be excessive, the root system will be overtaxed, and the plant will form too many crowns which in turn will militate against good performance in ensuing years. Reduction of the shoots to a single stem, or two at most, in the first season and to not more than five in any subsequent season will help materially to ensure good quality of spike, normal height, ease of staking and tying in an artistic way, and long life in the plant itself, anything from seven to ten years being quite common.

Of all the single attentions you can give to the plant this thinning is certainly the most important.

Staking and Tying

Our plant has many virtues, which have been outlined in Chapter 2 and elsewhere. They cannot be enjoyed, however, unless the plants are kept upright, and this has been a problem to a great many people for a great many years. Two factors go a long way towards solving it, one being this very thinning just described. It is quite clear that, unthinned, we may find as many as twenty stems on one plant; in that case bad weather is almost bound to bring disaster, because to deal individually with so many stems is well-nigh impossible. Reduced to five, or at most seven, the problem becomes simpler. The reduction prevents the plant from

21a. A five-year-old plant commencing vigorous spring growth, but needing to be thinned

21b. Commencing to reduce the stems by removing the slimmer ones, using a sharp knife and cutting outwards to obviate damage to the remaining stems

21c. Thinned down to well-separated stems, one to each crown

21d. The same plant ten days later, showing seven stems, one of which on the left still needs to be removed

e. Canes inserted, one to each stem, and the first or anchor tie being made

f. Cane inserted into the ground outside the point at which the stem emerges, so as not to damage the crown, but upright so that when tied the tie holds the stem back and prevents it spreading outwards

g. Six stems in full bloom, the canes nicely hidden by the foliage and the blooms well separated, thus permitting sun and air to harden the stems and preventing the plant becoming abnormally tall

63

growing abnormally tall; it also hardens the stems by letting the sun and air get at them and so there is less risk of breakage. As will be seen in Fig. 22, the use of twiggy pea-sticks is sometimes preferred, but on the whole this detracts greatly from the beauty of the plant.

Sometimes a method is used whereby the individual spikes are tied right up to the top (see Chapter 12 on Exhibiting), but the author does not think this can ever be seriously advocated for general garden use, which leads to the second factor. Obviously if one is unlucky enough to have a garden so wind-swept as to make this method of staking and tying essential then one should clearly avail oneself of the wide range of short and sturdy plants now available and avoid anything over 4 ft 6 ins. This introduction of plants flowering from 3 ft to 4 ft 6 ins. high gives the full answer in coastal districts and on windy sites. Named plants in this height category are available; probably by the time this book is published Blackmore and Langdon's short-growing seed strain will be available. The production of bigger and better delphiniums, culminating in the giant Commonwealth plants and such plants from Bath as 'Emir' and 'Great Scot', has been forced on breeders by popular clamour over the years; at the same time it has been the biggest single factor in dissuading thousands of gardeners from growing the plant, because they have considered them too big. Small gardens, small borders, and windswept sites cannot accommodate these giants, but these thousands now have the chance of enjoying their delphiniums to the full, and keeping them upright as well.

Apart from the height of the plant, my own favoured staking method of a medium to light cane per spike is illustrated in Figs. 21e–f. By means of thinning I always find it practicable to put a 4 ft cane to each stem and to have my plants reasonably upright and natural-looking at flowering time. The canes themselves are visible only for a matter of three weeks. Coupled with the use of a really thick soft string in making the ties, the ideal combination will result. A possible alternative, but perhaps less satisfactory method, is the placing of three canes to each plant, tying round the plant on the three canes, thus holding it in. This is less effective as it leaves the spikes swinging about too much.

22. Twiggy pea-sticks supporting delphiniums at Wisley

With experience, I find that only two ties per spike are necessary. One early, as seen in Fig. 21f, and one left as late as possible to be made just before the bottom florets open and at the highest point where the stem feels really sun-hardened, below the top foliage in any case. Once you have the anchor tie made there is no need to fear breakage until the flowers open, because they do not hold the added weight of rainwater while in bud.

The first, or anchor tie, is vital, and especially so with a few named kinds where the stems come out of the ground and tend to curve first outwards and then upwards. 'Anne Page', 'Jack Tar', and 'Blue Ice' are three like this; if not held in at an early stage they may well be spread-eagled before flowering.

Watering

For garden purposes thorough soil preparation of the kind indicated, followed year by year by constant summer hoeing, and the digging in of humus in winter, should be sufficient for mature plants in all but the hottest of summers. But these measures are not enough for young plants, seedlings, or rooted cuttings, or for transplanted plants; nor are they enough for mature plants if real drought sets in.

In the British Isles no watering of any kind should be contemplated until the plants are 18 ins. or so high. I give this instruction by height rather than by variable season. Not even in continued drought for the first 4–5 weeks of growth would I water, because the soil preparation plus thinning should be adequate to combat it. If the drought continued and I decided to do something about it I should make sure, above all else, that the water reached the area *below* the plants. Provided one has not allowed the situation to last too long and get out of hand, it is fairly easy to accomplish, but it does mean leaving one's sprinkler or spray lines in position for at least three hours to have any real effect. Two or three days after, or whenever the surface soil ceases to be muddy, the area is hoed to make a tilth, or a surface mulch of leaf-mould or something similar is applied, both steps being designed to cut the capillary channels by means of which the moisture is drawn upwards into the air.

Should there be sufficient drought to justify it I would repeat

66

this measure throughout the summer. Such conditions rarely apply in Great Britain but will be common in Johannesburg, Melbourne, parts of Kenya, and many parts of the U.S.A. where delphiniums nevertheless are successfully grown.

As to special feeding, this can be undertaken, if desired, from 12 ins. high up to the point where the buds begin to swell and take colour. This is further discussed in Chapter 12 which is primarily designed for exhibitors. For the garden, special feeding is not really necessary, provided the ground is adequately prepared and maintained.

Cultivation at Flowering Time

Beyond what has already been indicated there is little to do when the plants are in flower except to attend to the speedy removal of those spikes the florets on which have started dropping. At that stage where the spike has ceased to give a pleasant colour effect it should be cut off cleanly just below the bottom floret, so as to give the secondary side-spikes or laterals every opportunity of getting full nourishment and continuing the display (see Fig. 35). Quite apart from the fact that spikes left to go to seed look untidy, and quite overpower the flowering of the laterals, they are depriving the plant of energy and vigour to no good purpose. Each pod may well contain twenty seeds or so; to let all the pods set seed takes up a lot of energy which might otherwise go to the laterals, and if seed is required the need may be met by leaving just two or three pods at the base when removing the main spike.

In due time the laterals finish flowering and the flowering portions are removed in like manner, leaving the plant to die down naturally, which it does by October or thereabout.

Second Flowering

Plants sometimes send up shoots a second time; these are usually apparent by the end of July. If they come, nature may not be denied and the best course is to cut the old growth down to the ground as soon as the new shoots are observed, thus opening the 'new' plant up to sun and air. Concentrate then on letting the plant complete its natural cycle – that is, to flower and set seed – so as to prevent any possibility of a third set of shoots coming up only to be murdered by the onset of winter. To this end encourage these second shoots by reducing them to one (or two at most), thus channelling the nourishment into the one spike and ensuring it has time to stretch out and flower.

But mature plants do not normally send up second shoots. If they do not then I am opposed to cutting them down prematurely and forcing second growth by artificial watering, because it tends to shorten a plant's life, and autumn colours in delphiniums are apt to be unrepresentative anyway.

In either event, by the end of October our plants are ready to be cut down. Personally, I like this to be done as near ground level as possible to reduce the stagnant water in the hollow stumps over the winter. All that remains is to mulch the stool and immediate surround with coarse ash or grit as a deterrent to slugs, and to keep the ground clean throughout the winter.

Good and Bad Seasons

Nature provides variety. The gardener's task is to mould the conditions to the plants' needs. In a lucky season, where growth begins and proceeds without check, where nature provides the correct admixture of sun and rain and where perhaps the plants are in virgin soil, the gardener may be fortunate enough to grow good delphiniums with little trouble. In other and more normal seasons, faced by the vagaries of most climates, he can achieve a large measure of success by the methods indicated or adaptations of them.

By the way, don't try to grow delphiniums in shady spots. Remember, the plant is a sun-lover despite its water requirements and, if colour, hardness of stem, and height are to be normal, the plant must be fully in the open.

4 · Seed and seedlings

The seed itself, a sound method of germinating it, and the subsequent culture of the baby plants up to both first flowering (which never represents the plant's potential) and second flowering (which does) are portrayed in a series of pictures from Figs. 23a to 23u, 24a to 24d, and 25 to 34.

But first the virtues of seed and also its failings should be considered. It should be noted that seedlings are all essentially different in some respect or other; comparatively few in fact even look similar. Named plants are always true to the original seedling, of which they are virtually a part. As such, in a named plant you are purchasing a known quantity which has been tried and tested for at least five to seven years, probably much longer. You know what it will look like and you know its virtues because they are ascertainable. Also you know that the breeders had such a high opinion of the original seedling that they have gone through the laborious procedure of building up the stock, naming it, and listing it for sale; you also know that it is one of the very few survivors out of several thousands of seedlings raised over those seven years from hand-crosses made as a result of years and years of built-up knowledge. In other words, there is a negligible risk in buying it, whatever the price, and it must necessarily be a plant of the front rank, at least at the time of its introduction.

Seed must be harvested and stored correctly in the vitally necessary cool conditions which alone preserve its power to germinate. This seed referred to so far comes from general named collections at Bath and at Codsall. The plants from which the seed comes are turned over on a ten- to thirty-year basis; new and better plants come in after trial, and the least good are scrapped. This is a constant process. It means, as we have already seen, that the collections are improving annually. That in turn means that the potential from seed also increases annually, and that the seed itself must be worth sowing because it is virtually the next generation of the crosses which made the plants from which it is saved. As will be seen in Chapter 6 on Breeding for the Amateur, of the qualities which go to make up a plant some are readily inheritable and some appear less so : they are, as the breeders say, dominant and recessive, respectively.

All the top-rank delphinium seed harvested for sale is self-pollinated, or formed by natural means. While experiments have shown that flower seed from cross-pollinated flowers gives stronger seedlings than self-fertilized seed, the delphinium seedlings from natural seed of the two main British strains are vigorous enough to satisfy anyone. The construction of the procreative parts is such as to prevent pollination by bees and other insects and this has been proved and agreed at Bath, Codsall, and in California. Yet, as with groundsel which is similarly protected, there is no general or progressive lack of vigour in the resultant plants.

From the seed of the Blackmore and Langdon strain, and the Bishop and Commonwealth strains, all the good qualities noted so far, which are discussed further in later chapters and may be seen portrayed in many of the pictures, are obtainable. Some recessive qualities may also appear and in a small percentage of plants they may prove undesirable. Some seedlings may prove shorter-lived than others, though in the main this particular fault applies mostly to the plants of the Giant Pacific seed strain. Worthwhile plants will result from all three, plants of good form and good colour, new colour combinations, and, possibly, in the case of the two British strains, new plants worthy of introduction.

As to perenniality and longevity, those qualities which are rightly so precious in the herbaceous border, these are certainly dominants in the Bath strain where crossing and back-crossing to fix them has been going on for so many years. I think it fair to put the Codsall strains in second place on these counts, though there has been steady improvement through the years. The colour range from Codsall seed is immense and the strain possesses more of the unexpected in this regard than any. The Giant Pacifics, a poor third as perennials, have advantages; one is that they flower earliest of all and the other is that they can be purchased to flower to selected colours.

Lastly, the biggest advantage which all seed affords is its economy, which makes good delphiniums a possibility for all, in form and in quality which has never before been available. There is also great delight and pleasure to be had from raising this plant from seed.

Seed and Germination

If a packet of seed is kept in a drawer of a desk from harvest time until spring, germination will be nil. In these enlightened days valuable seed stocks are properly stored dry and cold at 35°–40° F., and if they have to be posted any distance involving heat in transit or at destination it is essential that Air Mail be used, otherwise germination may well be poor.

Owing to refrigeration there is no longer any need to fear poor germination and there are no special peculiarities about the sowing of the seed. Anyone can grow it successfully, whatever facilities may be lacking.

The Time to Sow

Undoubtedly the very best time to sow is immediately the seed is ripe. In England the season's seed is often available in August, certainly in September, and ripe seed obtained then will germinate in eight to fourteen days and as much as 95 to 100 per cent. The plants will be small by the onset of winter, however, and cold-frame protection at least will be necessary. They will need to be kept in the pots or the box at the stage shown in Figs. 23p and o, to die down in November–December and commence new growth in March before being planted out. In the set of pictures we have an early April sowing growing right on to flower in August. These plants will in the main not give representative spikes until June of the year after sowing, whereas autumn-sown seed will give main spikes the following late July–August, a matter of ten to eleven months in all.

For those who can provide warm conditions in a greenhouse in January it is possible to sow then for uninterrupted growth right through to representative flowering in September. This is common practice with Blackmore and Langdon and with Bakers of Codsall.

71

Normal sowing time for most gardeners coincides with the commencement of growing conditions in the spring, usually March, but either alternative is preferable if the facilities and the attention are available.

Sowing Conditions and Compost

The seed is small so a fine compost is a good thing for the top half-inch in any case, and rough materials should be avoided. A sterilized John Innes seedling compost, sieving the top half-inch, is satisfactory but one may also use one part horticultural vermiculite to two parts compost, and put a tablespoon of fine bone-meal to each seed box. The vermiculite helps to ensure against having to water again pending germination, and the bone-meal gives a greatly improved root system on the little seedlings.

The compost mixture is uniformly moist at sowing time, but *not soggy*. After sowing on the surface I sieve up to a quarter-inch of compost on to the seed, and then water it in once through a fine rose. As you see in Fig. 23b I place my seed boxes on the cinder floor of a cold frame, cover them with heavy quality polythene because the seed germinates better in the dark, and ventilate the frame well all day so as to prevent the temperature rising above 60°. At dusk I shut the lights to prevent the temperature of the compost dropping below 45–50° and am always ready to cover the lights with a tarpaulin to keep out severe frost. The polythene laid across the seed boxes ensures conservation of moisture while enabling the boxes to breathe and I have found that its use on a sterilized compost prevents the formation of white, woolly fungus and mossing over, both of which can be a nuisance.

Similar conditions can be produced in a greenhouse, or in a suitable garage window or living-room window-sill. It is only a matter of ingenuity and adaptation, and germination should be completed in fourteen days. It can easily be fatal to water the boxes during the first fourteen days. Whether polythene is used or not, every precaution should be taken to obviate any necessity for such watering. If it does appear vital, the lightest sprinkling possible should be given and the cover replaced.

23a. The ripened seed of the delphinium is golden-brown to black in colour, shiny and slightly shrivelled in appearance

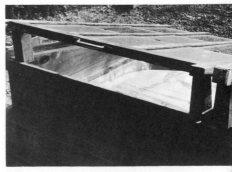

23b. Lights well open to keep down the daytime temperature, seed boxes insulated with polythene to preserve the proper state of moisture and to obviate repeated waterings

23c. Germination begins in fourteen days from sowing

23d. The polythene is transferred to the frame-light to keep hot sun off the tiny plants

23e. Close-up of seed leaves or cotyledons on the fourteenth day – note the seed-shells adhering to the tips of the cotyledons

23f. Mature cotyledons and young true leaves at pricking-on stage or potting-on stage

74

23g. Do not attempt to move these tiny plantlets until you have soaked and drained the seed boxes. Roots will be torn if you attempt potting up from dry boxes

23h. A typical seedling at the potting-up stage

23i. Inserting seedling into 3½-in. pot

23j. Firming up

23k. Potted up and ready for watering by immersion

23l. A weak solution of liquid seaweed in a galvanized container

23m. Pricking on from the stage depicted in Fig. 23h, an alternative to potting up

23n. Twelve seedlings pricked out into one box

23o. The same a few weeks later, showing the box filled with roots, and central shoots formed

23p. The potted-up plants at approxi-
ately the same stage as in Fig. 23o,
and ready for planting out

23q. Close up of one potted plant. Note
similarity to boxed plants in Fig. 23o

23r. The same plant knocked out of the
pot and showing a nice root system,
yet not so plentiful as to be pot-
bound. If left in the pot too long the
foliage will turn yellow and the plant
will be slow to get away when
planted

23s. Two to three weeks after planting, and obviously in very good health

23t. The young maiden spike has formed. Strong-minded gardeners will nip this off so as to promote the formation of a fat bud on the crown and a large and representative spike

23u. Most of us like to see the colour of our seedlings. Quite a nice variety here

24a. The single-petalled types sometimes turn up; they always wish to set seed too soon and do not adorn the garden for long

24b. However beautiful these florets may be the plant should be scrapped because the habit is too shy

The Young Plantlets

It is easy to watch for progress in germination and there will be minor upheavals in eight or nine days. Main germination takes fourteen days, however, and I wait for that before stripping off my polythene, which I then pin to the outside of the well-opened light in order to produce the slight shade and protection from the sun which is necessary to keep the temperature within bounds. If I did my work on a living-room window-sill I would polythene the window and open at the top for ventilation.

Within a further fortnight or so the true leaves will appear (see Fig. 23f) and the little plantlets will be ready for potting up singly or for pricking out into boxes (see Figs. 23i and 23m). Whether potted or boxed they need the same protection for a few days, that is, shaded lights well open. But as the plants begin to grow away and fill the pot, so the protection comes off, at first by day and latterly by night as well, until the point is reached

24c. Consistently ugly placement of florets

24d. Symmetrical placement, nicely formed florets, but far too widely spaced to give good colour effect. Note how the stem is visible almost the whole way up

where they are to be planted out (see Figs. 23p and q, and 23o). The gradual removal of protection is to accustom the plants to sun and air and frost, so that they receive no check on planting out.

During the whole time between germination and planting out daily attention is given to watering. Whilst the plants are gathering strength in the boxes after removal of the polythene this will constitute *a light sprinkling daily* through a fine rose. After potting up and watering by immersion each pot must receive individual attention each day, or a sprinkler or spray line be used, up to planting out.

In the Open

We have already prepared our ground thoroughly. If space is a consideration, and the best results are wanted, then it is advisable to see the colour, form, and height of the delphiniums before selecting favourites to put into the border proper. At this stage therefore one should usually plant the seedlings in rows in a nursery garden or piece of the vegetable plot, with 2 ft between rows and 9 ins. between plants. By the time the representative spikes have been seen, the relative merits can be assessed and the selection made. *It is impossible to judge by the first spike* which is always puny.

What to look for

Tastes differ as regards colour, the needs of the site in many cases govern the height of plant admissible, but there are plenty of points all should watch for.

There will be plants to flower early, and others to flower late, some will have slim and elegant stems, and some few may be fleshy and coarse. It is useless keeping any plants the florets of which are single; however attractive the colour the petals will not hold long and one is bound to be able eventually to find a similar colour in a long-lasting semi-double. Singles in these seed strains are very few and far between but do sometimes occur. As to form and placement of florets I think that those who study the plates in this book cannot fail to form a good idea of what to look for and what to avoid. The rest is a matter of personal taste.

These seedlings are being grown, it is assumed, for personal pleasure and garden effect. On that basis, high quality results can easily be obtained. For garden purposes we can admit of wider limits than for exhibition and the gaining of awards. Plants should have spikes of nice proportion with size of florets, length of spike, general height of plant all in keeping. Whether such spikes are 1 ft 6 ins.–2 ft long, or whether they have an exhibition 4 ft of bloom is not of paramount importance. Certainly an over-crowded spike is ugly and to be eliminated, but a somewhat loosely built spike often has an elegance and grace which appeals very much to gardeners of good taste whereas it would not please the show judges. As to height, generalizations are not possible but it must be a fact that plants from 3 ft to 4 ft 6 ins. or 5 ft will be eagerly sought after by the garden-minded. They will be readily found in all three seed strains; study of Chapters 8 and 13 will further demonstrate the possibilities of the seed which must

25. A good example in the bud stage of a broad based or pyramidal spike, made possible by long pedicels held at a less acute angle than in a columnar spike (see Figs. 30 and 34)

inherit to a high degree the desirable qualities of the named plants from which it is saved.

Florets and Bees

General study of many of our pictures, and especially Figs. 26, 27, 28, and 29 depicting a collection of florets, will make it clear that the variety of petal formation and of eye formation is very wide indeed. Petal colours are fully dealt with throughout the book, but the importance of the bee formation and colour is not always realized. They are available in white, cream, so extensively yellow-haired as to appear yellow, black and gold, all shades of brown from fawn to sepia, striped black and blue, white and blue, and many other combinations. Their shape is of infinite variety as well as their size. The importance of all this to the general effect created will be realized if you visualize two identical pale blue delphiniums, one with a white eye, one with a black eye. The colour effect created is entirely different. Then again there are eyes which are like small petals of the same colour as the main petals (see 'Elizabeth Schumann' in Fig. 43).

Slugs

Unfortunately one cannot write about delphiniums without mentioning slugs, and fairly fully at that. Those interested will find them fully dealt with in Chapter 7 on Pests and Diseases and can contemplate a very clear picture of one of these voracious beasts in Fig. 44a. If your seedlings are to flourish from germination onwards you *must* wage constant war against the slug.

Seedlings in Perspective

These comments may help the reader to evaluate named varieties and seedlings; if I were to suppose that I had retained my delphinium knowledge but had no plants, possibly my conclusions in this situation will be of use.

Firstly, were money no object, I should buy an extensive collection from the varieties selected in Chapter 13. Secondly, if reasons of economy compelled me to disregard all post-war plants, I certainly would not purchase plants introduced more than twenty years ago, because modern seed would give results

26. Formation of petals and corolla vary greatly, as well as colour

far superior to varieties which would be virtually obsolete with perhaps a few exceptions. Thirdly, if possible, I should certainly have both the named plants of known perfection and also the seed with its excitements and pride of raising.

27. Formation of petals and corolla vary greatly, as well as colour

28. Formation of petals and corolla vary greatly, as well as colour

29. The florets here and in Figs. 26, 27, and 28, have not been selected for size. They are good average modern florets from the middle of the spike

30. A nice colum-
    nar seedling
    of average size

31. A short-growing seedling of palest lavender. Beautiful floret placement, good healthy foliage, but a trifle squat at the tip.

32. A nicely formed seedling when mature – note the lovely straight
and slender stem and the plentiful laterals

33. This seedling was exceptionally early to flower, basal florets were within 12 ins. of the ground, laterals and main stem were slim but particularly hard

34. Another well-formed
early-flowering type
with nice flat, formal
flowers

35. All garden plants, to be satisfactory, should have a good supply of
strong laterals. The main spike has been removed as soon as the
flowers dropped, thus directing the plant's energies into the laterals

94

36. Not a particularly strong plant but a good one for illustration,
    showing willingness to flower

5 · Division and cuttings

Most gardeners purchase plants or raise them from seed, to be left alone in the border for the whole of their useful life. With the delphinium this can be anything from five to twenty years with regular thinning and cultivation, for it is very hardy indeed. However, there are occasions when a plant has special appeal and the owner wishes to have more of it. There are only two ways in which the stock of any given delphinium can be increased, by dividing it into pieces each with its own crown and roots, or by removing the shoots in early spring, inserting them in a suitable compost in a closed propagating box, and causing the shoots to emit roots from the base. It is of course necessary to be able to propagate a given plant if gardening is to be really interesting and economical, and this chapter provides those interested with the means of succeeding.

Division

Lifting a plant out of the ground either in autumn or in early spring and chopping it into pieces with a downward stroke of the spade or putting two forks into it back to back and prising it apart, these are normal methods with herbaceous plants. Neither is to be commended for our plant because the worn-out part of the crown in the centre is still being replanted and that is not only useless but also may be very unhealthy. As with michaelmas daisies, phlox, and other plants, the healthy and vigorous crowns on the delphiniums are around the outside of the stool. They are the pieces which should be separated and replanted. It is strongly advised therefore that when the stool has been lifted it should be washed clean so that one can see exactly what one is doing. There is a good picture of a plant so washed in Fig. 37c. After washing it was seen that this was a particularly healthy plant with little dead matter in it. With a sharp knife cutting downwards from above, this plant offered obvious points between the previous season's stems where complete division was possible and it made five, perfectly healthy divisions as the following picture will show.

37a. A plant entering its fifth season and getting a little unwieldy

37b. The same plant, lifted for division

37c. Washed clean with the hose to facilitate division

37d. Five nice divisions, one of which is being replanted in Fig. 19c

It should be noted that shoots mostly spring from the crown all round the outer circumference of the old season's stems. This is a natural habit and enough has been said to show that haphazard methods of division are inadvisable. Of course there are instances in which a lifted plant falls to pieces by reason of the presence of rot in the crown; in this event no parts of the crown are likely to be healthy. In Fig. 38e a case is shown where this rot has penetrated down through the old cut-down stumps and up into the new season's shoots; in cases like these any kind of propagation is a waste of time, because the divisions are in poor health from the start.

A word must be said about the age of plants suitable for division. In general the older the plant the more likely it is that the organic tissues will have collapsed through age, thus causing the blackening referred to. The darker varieties do not seem to have such hard resistant crowns as the lighter shades, which latter are much less susceptible to this spreading internal collapse. If a plant has been created by rooting a cutting or from seed, the crown is not normally big enough by the spring of its second season to permit of satisfactory division. It can be done at a pinch, but entails a cut down through the middle of the maiden stem. It is far better to give such a plant one more season's cultivation, which will make all the difference and give much more scope. With plants from three to ten years old, of the best modern types, division should be practicable, but in the wetter and heavier soils an increasing proportion of rot may tend to be found in certain varieties and shades, especially purples, deep violets, and even in some cases dark blues.

As a matter of interest the plant which forms the subject of our picture series on division was a five-year-old seedling of pale silvery mauve, the crown of which was very yellow and extremely solid and hard. Such crowns are definitely harder, heavier and less fleshy than those of dark shades.

Cuttings

To give real point to the comparison between division and cuttings it should be stated that the plant which gave the five divisions shown in Fig. 37d had a minimum of thirty shoots each of which

98

could have been taken as a cutting to make a young and extremely healthy plant with a brand-new root system all its own. Those interested may like to study the picture series from Fig. 38a to s. In particular, Fig. 38c will give a clear idea of the size and appearance of a good cutting. And when it is further stated that plants grown from cuttings will as a general rule give far finer results than those from divisions in the season afterwards, it will be seen that there is really no comparison between the two methods for effectiveness.

As far as named varieties are concerned it frequently takes five years of trial and propagation before stocks are sufficient to permit sale. If division were the only means it might well take twenty years; with some varieties it would be impossible. This practice of taking cuttings was not general in Great Britain until Charles Langdon adopted it and made it known to other raisers, including Frank Bishop and Watkin Samuel; as a matter of interest M. Victor Lemoine's grandson informs me that *coutures d'yeux* were common practice with his father and grandfather at Nancy.

If cuttings are to be taken they must be completely healthy, of a length between 2 ins. and 5 ins. and absolutely solid across the cut base. Exposure of the pith or hollow, or signs of brown or black in the base mean that the cutting is useless and should be discarded (Fig. 38e).

Any excess foliage should be cut neatly off because it is only an added burden to the cutting during the period in which it has no roots, and the cutting itself must then be inserted in a rooting compost or medium and be enclosed in an atmosphere buoyant enough to keep it fresh and strong for upwards of three weeks until the roots are formed.

Irritant materials such as sharp sand, coal dust, ground pumice, vermiculite, and many others down to ordinary garden soil, have been used successfully to root cuttings in. Similarly, there are many ways in which such cuttings may be kept close for the necessary period; many have their own favourite means of doing these things. For instructional purposes I shall confine myself to the method best suited to the average week-end gardener. I choose a wooden box 12 in. deep, and not

38a. A plant entering its
     third season, lifted to
     facilitate the taking of
     cuttings. Note direc-
     tion of cut, down-
     ward and slightly *in-
     ward* as the shoots
     tend to curve in to-
     wards the crown

38b. The cut base and the
     cut crown, both com-
     pletely healthy, as
     well as solid

38c. Five fine cuttings, trimmed ready for insertion

38d. This cutting, taken too far away from the crown, has the hollow in the shoot exposed and will rot off quickly if you attempt to root it

38e. This plant looked healthy until the cut was made. The rot in the crown, which starts inside the base of the old stem has penetrated to the new growth. It is useless to attempt to root such cuttings

38f. Showing the maximum depth to which cuttings are inserted in the vermiculite. The clay pan seen here and in ensuing pictures is a good container for rooting under the closed lights of a shaded frame as it obviates waste of space

38g. Showing the deep box and sheet of glass method discussed in the text

38h. Daily inspection reveals a stem rotting

38i. The rotted shoot must be removed immediately

38j. The cuttings look and feel as if rooting has begun, so we test them

38k. Two cuttings reveal commencement of rooting, but hardly enough for potting-up so we insert them again and wait a little longer

381. A week later the roots have taken firm hold on the vermiculite and can be lifted with a ball, by the careful exercise of a steady lift

38m. Well rooted in the fourth week, and now being potted up for hardening off prior to planting out

38n. Normal potting-up method, very similar to the planting of the transplanted plant in Fig. 19c

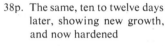

38o. Firming up, to be followed by watering by immersion and insertion into a cold frame for gradual hardening

38p. The same, ten to twelve days later, showing new growth, and now hardened

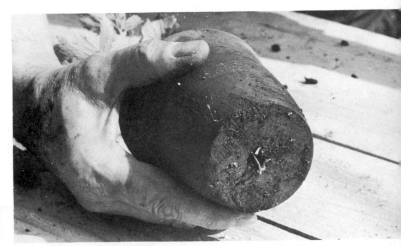

38q. Sure sign that the plant has a sufficient root system

38r. Here it is

38s. The main stem has its tip removed at planting time, thus inducing formation of new eyes on the crown. Two of these are shown coming up

more than 12 ins. across and 18 ins. long, as the container because it is manageable, can be lifted and moved about, and is easily closed either by a sheet of horticultural glass or by heavy quality polythene.

In the bottom of this box drainage holes are drilled with a red-hot poker, the holes are crocked, the box is lined with a half-inch depth of coarse weathered coke ashes and then topped up with a $3\frac{1}{2}$-in. depth of horticultural vermiculite. As everyone knows the grains of vermiculite have the useful property of holding water inside them like a sponge, while permitting the compost to breathe. This property is particularly useful for our purpose and for the week-end gardener because it means that if the box is sited properly there need be no question of any extra watering until the cuttings have actually formed roots.

Any form of heat will be resented by these cuttings and excessive dryness plus sunshine will mean certain death, because they will shrivel. Excessive watering and constant saturation of the small amount of air in the propagating box will also entail failure because it will mean beads of condensation on the leaves of the cuttings. In these matters a happy medium must be arrived at. It is done by soaking the vermiculite in water for eight hours to ensure saturation, then packing it down firmly into the box, not rammed tight and not loose. Allow the box to drain for two or three hours and then it is ready for use.

The cuttings may be inserted 2 ins. apart, with 3 ins. between rows; not more than 1 in. of the cutting should be inserted. Firm moderately on insertion but not hard enough to damage the tissues at the base. After filling the box and before putting the glass into position, leave the box open in a hut or garage for a couple of hours to ensure that the top growth of the cutting is bone dry. *This is very important*. The covered box should then be placed in full light but never exposed to direct sunshine. It should be in a handy spot, like a garage shelf, unheated room, or out-building where it is protected from snow, hail, and heavy rain, thus facilitating the small amount of attention needed. This consists of turning the glass at dusk to get rid of condensation, covering with sacking for the night to maintain a minimum of 45°, removing in the morning and turning the glass once more.

On no account should the temperature be allowed to rise above 60°, the feel of the surface of the vermiculite to the finger should remain cool and moist, never dry, and I repeat that if the operation is carried out successfully these conditions can easily be fulfilled. Inside the first week the tips of the cuttings will begin to open and by the end of the second week of closed conditions the appearance will be fresh and green and the tops of the cuttings will feel very firm and alive to a light finger touch. Keep trimming any dying leaves with sharp scissors and do not allow such foliage to droop on to the surface of the vermiculite because a woolly fungus will result and may spread.

In the third and fourth weeks inspect the cuttings carefully once each day for dying foliage and blackening stems, both of which must be carefully removed (see Figs. 38h and i). By the end of the third week some cuttings will have the appearance of having rooted, the centres showing new and bright green growth. This is usually an illusion so far as roots are concerned, but quite a normal procedure otherwise. Early in the fourth week, test some of the cuttings daily; you will find rooting is beginning, and a peep at Figs. 38j, k, l, and m will help you to understand the situation.

When rooting in the box is judged to be general the box may be given a quick immersion in water at about 50°. This eases removal and the plantlets themselves must then be potted up in a manured potting mixture since the vermiculite is, of course, sterile and devoid of nourishment. If it is inconvenient to pot up immediately, the box should be given a quick immersion in diluted fertilizer and then left in its original position *but with the glass removed altogether*. Testing for rooting and speedy removal of this cover are important because although rooted there still remains a danger of top growth damping off if kept close for too long.

Up to this stage, through being grown in close conditions, the young plants are soft and tender. They must be hardened before being planted out in the open, as with the potted-up seedlings. A cold frame is useful for this purpose but in its absence the difficulty can easily be overcome with a few boards or bricks and a lath frame covered with polythene. Hardening off should not take more than eight–ten days, and so we have our new plants planted out into well-prepared ground a matter of six to seven weeks after taking the cuttings. The rest is just a matter of keeping the hoe going, stopping the plant by nipping off the bud when formed, thus compelling an immediate extension of the root action. This in turn induces eye formation on the crown and up come the new shoots (see Fig. 38s) to be treated in like manner in due course. The young delphinium is a plant which responds very quickly to the finger and thumb, plus the hoe.

As we have already seen in Chapter 3, all that remains is to allow the early August shoots to come up, thinning them to one and allowing this one to flower and even to set seed. This ensures a fine healthy crown, well supplied with fat but dormant buds to lie low in preparation for a truly representative display the following season and for many years thereafter. A sound foundation has been laid; the rest will follow.

I have outlined a method which is proved and sure. Follow it exactly, or improvise on similar lines, and you should succeed. There are other methods such as taking half-inch eyes and a slice of crown and setting them 2 ins.–3 ins. deep, and even layering, by means of a nick or cut at the base of a stem 12 ins. tall and packing the soil back again to await root formation before severing or separating. These methods do not contend seriously with the method advised.

As for the latest technique of all, mist propagation, I have always felt instinctively that it cut across the basic principle of *keeping the visible parts of the cuttings completely dry during the period of root formation.* My whole experience of damping off in many years of propagation has taught me to associate it with an over-moist atmosphere or with conditions where condensation is so great as to make it drip from the glass on to the cutting, or where the limited air is so saturated that it can hold no more and the excess, of necessity, settles on the foliage and stems. The least sign of anything like this happening must be treated as the precursor of failure and action must at once be taken to dry off the top growth, to place the propagating box in a cooler spot and to insulate better at night. An experiment in mist technique was conducted at Wisley by Mr Francis Hanger, Curator of the

111

39. Francis Hanger, the Curator of the R.H.S., Wisley Gardens, doing some first-aid to a plant in the Delphinium Trials

112

Royal Horticultural Society's Wisley Gardens, in the spring of 1958. As a matter of interest, and for the record, of 200 cuttings treated by mist technique in a propagation house at temperatures of 55–60° all but twenty-two were completely rotted off in twenty-one days; a batch of one hundred treated at 45–50° showed partial rooting in eight days and 100 per cent rooting in twenty-one days, whereas a control of a hundred cuttings, in sand, peat, and loam without mist and set in a well drained cold frame and a tight top, showed rooting beginning twenty-one days after insertion, followed by a hundred nice sturdy little plants by the thirty-fourth day, each with a very strong root system. An extract from Mr Hanger's notes reads as follows:

It will be observed that the least successful results were obtained where there were conditions of high temperature and humidity and the best results in the colder and less humid conditions. The best batch of cuttings was undoubtedly that rooted in the cold frame, and it would seem that this method is to be preferred for amateur gardeners.

At Bath, where new techniques are usually tested, mist propagation was successful but it is generally agreed that the method is quite unnecessary for the delphinium and for the amateur.

Lastly, it must be repeated that propagation by cuttings or by division is not a general necessity. Those who do not undertake it can enjoy their plants for many years and there is no question of having to renew the stock in order to preserve the standard and quality. Increase is only for those who want more of a good thing, or for specialist exhibitors.

6 · Breeding for the Amateur

A previous chapter has dealt with the raising of seedlings for garden purposes from seed which has been provided by nature, that is, self-fertilized or selfed seed. As you know, high-class results can now be obtained by these means. Additionally line-breeding has reached a very high standard, yet there is still plenty of scope for the amateur to provide something new and desirable. My main purpose here, therefore, is to give the interested few who may wish to make a cross or two the benefit of the best known guiding principles, and to give to all a new insight into the complexities, difficulties, and disappointments of line-breeding with such hybrid stock as the *elatum* delphiniums.

Each single delphinium plant has many valued characteristics, such as colour, size of floret, thickness of petal, length of spike, overall stature, foliage, stem, form and proportion of plant, resistance to mildew, ease of propagation, vigour and perenniality, and so on. To the specialists no plant is yet perfect, and the delphinium is no exception. Amongst your seedlings or your named plants you are never likely to find one which satisfies the highest critical standard in every single aspect. If it were so that would be an end to progress. You are much more likely to find plants which to you have some really outstanding virtue, coupled with a fault or faults. We should remind ourselves that for every named plant which has proved a valued breeder there are probably half-a-dozen unknown seedlings which have played an important part in their pedigree. If, for instance, we could refer to the pedigree of all the plants in our selections in Chapter 13 we should not be much the wiser because they would mostly be unnamed varieties known only by a number in the stud book, and which have never been distributed.

And this is the sort of thing that happens to breeders, whether professional or amateur, whether line-breeding or just making an occasional cross. They become faced with a seedling which, while it has faults, has also a really noteworthy quality in some respect or other. Should this happen, then the opportunity should be taken to breed this outstanding quality into a plant which has not the same faults. Thus you have two plants, the virtues of which could, if united, complement each other and form a well-nigh perfect individual. Of these two plants one must act as the female or seed-bearer and the other will be the male or pollen-parent.

Most amateurs decide on their crosses one year and effect them the next, as soon as the plants are ready, and it is usual to use the basal florets as the female parent because they are the first to be ready. It is quite possible, however, to effect a cross higher up the spike or even on the laterals, and this can have the advantage of gaining a year. In California Frank Reinelt has no choice since his plants are not retained for a second season: most of his crosses have to be made high up on the spike or on the laterals because the parents cannot be selected until they are open enough to be judged for quality. At Bath also, many crosses are made on the laterals.

Pollen, which is contained in the anthers of a flower (see Fig. 40d), is potent and carries with it all the qualities of the plant from which it comes. It is essential therefore to remove the pollen from the female parent or seed-bearer before it is free, for otherwise it will set its own seed and no cross will be possible. The picture series from Fig. 40a shows how this is done. At the time the immature anthers are removed the female and receptive part of the flower, known as the stigma, will not be visible. Anther removal speeds its growth and the stigma, sticky and receptive, is usually there in about four days. There remains to carry to the stigma the pollen of the male parent; this is best done in the calm conditions of a dry morning, and repeated, as an insurance against failure, once or even twice on successive days. Our pictures should make the matter clear.

The cross is made and the seed is fertilized; the pods swe_ ripen. Before they crack open on their own, at about the shown in Fig. 40i, it is sound policy to tie a small muslin sq round and underneath in order to make sure that the bird not get the seed, which the bullfinches love. When the pods l browned and opened, cut off the whole head of seeded pods, l it upside down and shake it into the muslin.

40a. A single floret at the stage at which emasculation should take place – i.e. before its pollen is free to effect natural fertilization

40b. Opened up to show the corolla – little petals with the shiny green-black pollen-bearing anthers nestling in the centre

40c. Pulling off the corolla petals with finger and thumb

40d. Leaving anthers only, to be removed with light but firm twist with finger and thumb

40e. Emasculation complete, this is the appearance the spike will have, its upper and unwanted part, together with all laterals, having been cut off

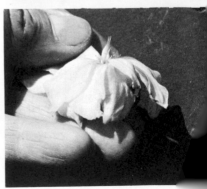

40f. Four or five days later the pistils and stigmas have grown and the stigmas are receptive

117

40g. Pollen of male parent on to stigmas of female parent

40h. Pollen clearly adhering to stigmas, thus ensuring fertilization

40i. A few weeks later all but three sets of pods reveal that the cross has been successful. Time to protect with muslin before the birds do damage

Sown immediately, the seed will germinate speedily and completely. Flower on these first-generation seedlings will be available twelve months after sowing the seed, and you may then find that some of the good qualities from both parents are present, that some good qualities are not there, and that faults still persist. Virtues and faults which are present in the first generation of seedlings from the cross are known as 'dominants', virtues and faults which are absent are called 'recessive'. A possible course to pursue is to save self-fertilized seed from the best plant or two of this first batch and to sow it. In this second generation a greater percentage of success may be observed a twelve-month hence at flowering time; by that is meant that the general average of resemblance to the original parents will have risen, and thus it is in the grandchildren that success will often be found. Success, of course, means finding a plant or plants in which the original virtues of the grandparents are allied and the faults dropped or cast aside. A third and even a fourth generation may be attempted, but a much more usual step at first- or second-generation stage would be to select the best plant and to cross it with one or other of the original plants, the grandparents. This will, selectively, have the effect of giving an added injection of the correct blood, according to the qualities which are missing. This is known as back-crossing and is widely employed.

Good form and habit, strength and vigour and proportion are almost a *sine qua non* in a desirable plant. Colour, size, and shape of floret, plus bee variation are the qualities which will appeal most to the eye. The breeding of a particularly pretty fawn eye on to a lovely mid-blue delphinium, in place of the rather poorly formed and insignificant eye with which it is possibly handicapped, may well attract a breeder. Another plant may be so attractive that its proneness to the disfiguring mildew tempts the owner to cross it with a known and vigorous mildew-free plant in the hope, eventually, of discarding the disease, whilst maintaining the beauty. These hypothetical cases, and many other desirable combinations present themselves in every garden where delphiniums are grown. Nearly all are capable of achievement, given the necessary interest and patience, and resolve unshaken in the face of failures which are bound to occur. For it cannot be

41. Interesting petal
formation and
enlarged corolla
in Seedling
M6/54 in the
garden of Mr
H. R. N.
Rickett at Pir-
bright in Surrey

made too clear that there are no set formulae for success, only guiding principles.

A great deal of information on general breeding topics has been made available to me by Allan Langdon and by Frank Reinelt; some has been made use of at different points already but much that remains is of direct interest at this point, together with some small experiences of my own.

As an instance of an actual and exceptional plant turning up among seedlings – and such 'breaks' are frequently the fore-runner of new lines of achievement – I found a seedling in September 1958 which had definitely yellow buds which swelled up to a large size. I knew from this that it would be a large-flowered cream and that the placement and shape of spike was pleasing, but the outstanding thing about it was its foliage. Instead of being sickly yellow, shiny and curled up at the edges as the foliage of cream and yellow seedlings usually is, this was completely healthy and remained so. I duly saved a little self-fertilized seed and put out eight seedlings in 1959, in the spring of which year I also took three cuttings to increase the stock a little so as to help with experimentation. Of the seedlings one flowered cream, two white, one deep Parma-violet, and four pale mauve. Whites and creams are recessive colours normally so this was above averagely good, and I noted that all eight plants, including two whites and one cream, had good and mildew-free foliage. There remains now to cross the new cream back on to the original cream in an endeavour to fix the colour in the progeny; and if results at any time show a recession to poor foliage I shall make an entirely fresh start by crossing the healthy original with a strong-growing perennial white from another source. Per-sistence is essential to success and, as Frank Reinelt remarked, 'The more generations of fine parentage that can be piled up behind, the higher the percentage of the result.'

At the same time I had also asked Mr Reinelt how he set about breeding a new line of Giant Pacifics with fawn-coloured bees, this colour being soft and attractive. His reply was that in order to obtain seed that would come fawn-eyed he crossed two fawn bees, selected the most successful pair of seedlings and crossed them again, thus gradually creating a predominance of fawn in

42. A close-up to show the type of corolla Mr Rickett is breeding

the bees. An earlier chapter has shown how he bred a black eye
to his all-white plants to create the Percival series. The guiding
principles seem to remain standard really, and results depend
upon knowledge, selection, and the particular objective.

Nevertheless, valuable natural 'breaks' or mutations occur, as
well as disappointments and no better example could possibly
be found than in the pedigree of that very fine plant, 'Blue Jade',
in which figures a plant called 'Blue Tit' (see Fig. 70). I thought
that a plant's pedigree containing a good number of named
plants would itself afford fine material, from which many
interesting observations could be made and inferences drawn,
and in response to my request Allan Langdon has given us the
benefit of a particularly informative pedigree, part of which is
reproduced on page 124.

43. A very unusual floret with three clear sets of petals and a corolla made up of more petals, the whole being one shade of amethyst, with no other colour at all. This is 'Elizabeth Schumann', bred by C. R. Wootton of Bloxwich in Staffordshire

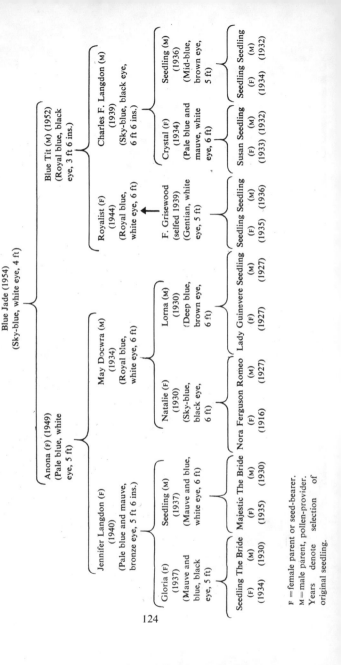

Blue Jade (1954)
(Sky-blue, white eye, 4 ft)

Anona (F) (1949)
(Pale blue, white eye, 5 ft)

Blue Tit (M) (1952)
(Royal blue, black eye, 3 ft 6 ins.)

Jennifer Langdon (F) (1940)
(Pale blue and mauve, bronze eye, 5 ft 6 ins.)

May Docwra (M) (1934)
(Royal blue, white eye, 6 ft)

Royalist (F) (1944)
(Royal blue, white eye, 6 ft) ←

Charles F. Langdon (M) (1939)
(Sky-blue, black eye, 6 ft 6 ins.)

Gloria (F) (1937)
(Mauve and blue, black eye, 5 ft)

Seedling (M) (1937)
(Mauve and mauve, white eye, 6 ft)

Natalie (F) (1930)
(Sky-blue, black eye, 6 ft)

Lorna (M) (1930)
(Deep blue, brown eye, 6 ft)

F. Grisewood (selfed 1939)
(Gentian, white eye, 5 ft)

Crystal (F) (1934)
(Pale blue and mauve, white eye, 6 ft)

Seedling (M) (1936)
(Mid-blue, brown eye, 5 ft)

Seedling	The Bride	Majestic	The Bride	Nora Ferguson	Romeo	Lady Guinevere	Seedling	Seedling	Seedling	Susan	Seedling	Seedling	Seedling
(F)	(M)	(F)	(M)	(F)	(M)	(F)	(M)	(F)	(M)	(F)	(M)	(F)	(M)
(1934)	(1930)	(1935)	(1930)	(1916)	(1927)	(1927)	(1927)	(1935)	(1936)	(1933)	(1932)	(1934)	(1932)

F = female parent or seed-bearer.
M = male parent, pollen-provider.
Years denote selection of original seedling.

124

Mr Langdon's comments on this pedigree point out that with its parents, 'Royalist' and 'Charles F. Langdon' at 6 ft and 6 ft 6 ins. respectively, the height of 'Blue Tit', which is only 3 ft 6 ins., is a definite break, possibly a natural mutation. He says, however, that the female grandparent, 'F. Grisewood', has a dwarfing tendency in cultivation despite its normal 5 ft. It is itself a fine blue; when first flowered in 1939 it was one of the best of its kind, and in breeding its blue colour has been found to be dominant above average.

It will be seen that at Bath the breeders have been swift to exploit the dwarfness and quality of 'Blue Tit'. It was crossed immediately on to 'Anona' and its dwarfness has been fairly dominant, producing not only 'Blue Jade' itself (see Fig. 62) but also the mid-blue 'Bebe', height 4 ft. The three semi-dwarfs are in fact the advance guard of an all-important new race of named plants and of a new seed strain which, flowering at 3 ft–4 ft should bring shorter delphiniums within the reach of everyone – a fine illustration of the best use possible being made of a worth-while development.

It is interesting to note that 'Blue Tit' owes its colour to its female parent and its eye to the male parent. With its son 'Blue Jade', the colour comes from the mother, eye as well, and the same is the case with another plant of the same cross, 'Bebe'. Both owe their dwarfness to 'Blue Tit', and the pollen parent was, in fact, dominant in the whole of the seedlings in this cross.

Another point with an important bearing on longevity is the degree of resistance to that debilitating disease, mildew. In this pedigree can be noted the rich blue 'Lorna'. Now this plant always was a bad mildew subject but its marriage to 'Natalie', producing mildew-free 'May Docwra', itself to be married to a plant immune to mildew, led to mildew-free progeny in both 'Anona' and 'Blue Jade'. The distaff side has been dominant here, while on the male side of 'Blue Jade's' family tree its immediate male parent 'Blue Tit' is practically immune, as are both its male grandparents, 'Royalist' and 'Charles F. Langdon'. And so, you see, 'Blue Jade' is altogether a very successful piece of breeding; with 'Bebe' as its sister, even more so. Clarity of colour, and blue at that, ideal height, unquestionable vigour

125

(again see Fig. 62), and mildew-resistance into the bargain. Added to which, its potential is by no means exhausted yet.

An attraction to those who like to save a little self-fertilized seed from a fine named plant is that the famous plant 'Royalist' came from selfed seed of 'F. Grisewood'. Many of the named plants give seedlings of good quality, some, such as sky blue 'Watkin Samuel' and gentian 'Mrs Frank Bishop', come very true to both colour and form. That lovely blue 'Blue Rhapsody' has a fragile stem prone to damage in high winds; a characteristic which unfortunately has proved dominant in heredity.

Enough has been said to illustrate the possibilities and the pitfalls. If a good plant turns up, its possibilities should be exploited, but there can never be any set formula for success and the unexpected does happen. With plants as hybrid as these, reversions occur at times; these may result in single-petalled plants, bad mildew subjects, small flowers, coarse and over-large stems, and so on. These are the occasional disappointments which breeders must face stoically. Lastly, anyone can enjoy the excitement of making an odd cross or two, but if serious line-breeding is to be attempted the plants have to be studied long and carefully, records have to be kept, knowledge built up and used intelligently. Above all, that innate sixth sense has to be developed.

7 · Pests and diseases

The delphinium is an extremely hardy plant and is not seriously prone to disease. Of garden pests, only one represents any real threat, and that is of course the slug.

Slugs and Snails

If a garden is slug-ridden, delphiniums will present these pests with a constant supply of food. They will eat the young seedlings as they germinate, the young shoots as they come up in the spring, and the dormant eyes below soil level before spring brings them up. It is absolutely essential to deal systematically with slugs and snails if the plants are to be a success.

Preventives fall into two classes, those which poison and those which kill on contact. Of the former, metaldehyde is the one commonly used and most effective. Although it can be obtained in liquid form it is more usual to mix it with attractive bran, placing it at strategic points round the plants, and renewing as necessary. The slaughter can be immense, but it must be pointed out that the mixture is definitely attractive to slugs and not repellent, nor does it stop the slug from breeding in the treated soil at a later date.

The only known contact-killer is a proprietary mixture sold in powder form, but readily soluble. It is said to have a form of alum in it, which being an astringent dehydrates the slug, thus killing it. Some gardeners make successful use of a dilution of sulphate of aluminium in a safe proportion ascertained by experiment. I have myself used the proprietary brand of contact-killer for many years, using it in liquid form direct on to the plants in December–February in open weather, and dusted round the plants weekly in March–May. It is important to attend to the base of hedges and to other daytime hiding-places as well as to the plants themselves. The contact-killer has two advantages; firstly, it does not in itself attract slugs to the neighbourhood of the plants, and secondly, it definitely deters slugs from breeding in the soil which has been treated, so that systematic usage can

44a. The large black field slug

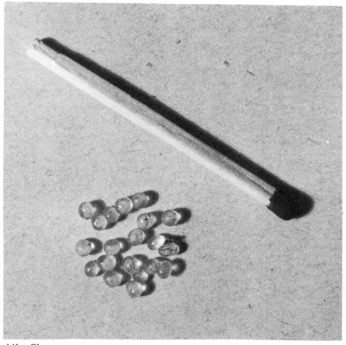

44b. Slug spawn

keep the plant slug-free. Used liquid in winter its main virtue is to kill the slugs which are deep down in the stool of the plant. It is also claimed that it dehydrates the clusters of eggs which are below surface level (see Fig. 44b).

As regards protection of seedlings, I usually water my frame heavily with a solution of contact-killer, then dust the surface, repeating regularly both inside and outside the frame, and similar precautions have to be taken in and around boxes or frames containing cuttings. Other sensible precautions against slugs consist of using sharp grit or ashes as a mulch round the crowns of plants from autumn to spring, also the floor of the cold frame. A recent discovery in New Zealand shows that an extensive 4-in. to 5-in. moisture-retaining mulch of sawdust will keep the plants immune because the slugs and snails cannot make progress over it.

Gardeners should also remember that the hedgehog and the Coach and Horses beetle eat slugs.

Caterpillars

In Figs. 45c and d may be seen a collection of moth larvae. These belong to the *Tortrix* moth, *T. cnephasia*, are about ¾ in. in length, coloured shiny olive-green with black spots, and plain dark brown. This moth is on the wing in May and the delphinium is one of its host plants. It lays its eggs amongst the budded spikes, for the larvae to hatch out seven days later and spin themselves homes either in the buds or in a tender young leaf. Later these same larvae go down and over-winter in the hollow cut-down stems, coming up again in March and April to repeat the process. As their favourite food is the young bud at the stage shown in Fig. 45a they can cause quite a lot of disappointment in spoiled spikes, and a close watch should be kept for the rolled up leaf in April and May, when hand-picking is sufficient for control.

In the autumn *the stems should be cut down to ground level*. By these means and by maintaining the use of the hoe these larvae can be fully controlled.

Millipedes, Leatherjackets, and Woodlice

Such pests are not primarily interested in the delphiniums and do

45a. A young leaf is stuck to the right-hand side of the embryo spike –
this spells danger

45b. Pulled apart, the leaf is seen to be eaten

45c. Tortrix moth larva is the culprit – if undetected the young buds
would have been chewed up

45d. A few larvae at different growth stages

46. Mildew

not cause damage to healthy plants in the open. It is only when rotted that the plant attracts them; they, and others including the moth larvae, are usually to be found in the stubble of a herbaceous border and if it so happens that a delphinium plant begins rotting they soon find a way into it to complete the job. The delphinium does have its own particular species of eelworm, known as *Pratylenchus pratensis*, which can attack the roots and stool of the delphinium direct, thus causing initial damage which can be worsened by millipedes and by stagnant water.

Mildew

The presence of the spores which carry and spread this disfiguring disease is usually not manifest until late July when foliage covered as in Fig. 46 may be observed. As winter approaches the spores assume a different form for protective purposes and so live and multiply. Spraying with lime-sulphur in mid-July is a good preventive and there are several proprietary sprays, but the best way of combating this ugly disease is to breed or grow varieties the foliage of which resists the spores. In this the breeders have been markedly successful, so that modern named varieties are generally resistant to it.

Gardeners should refrain from planting near or under trees, where humidity and closeness of atmosphere tend to prevail, nor should they retain the minority of seedlings which show themselves to be susceptible.

Delphinium foliage, apart from varying in colour from light green to dark green, also varies in its 'hairiness'. Some foliage is covered with a soft down and stems are quite prickly to the touch, others are shiny and hairless with smooth stems. While, on the whole, it may be said that the hairy stems and leaves are more receptive to the mildew spores and the smooth ones less susceptible, it is certainly not a general rule; exceptions in plenty may be found in both instances. It is also established that the dark purples, and some few of the dark blues, are more prone than the lighter colours, but it seems that hairiness and depth of colour are of very secondary importance. It is Allan Langdon's view that research directed towards the degree of acidity or alkalinity of the cell sap might be more fruitful. Dr Brian Langdon's view is that susceptibility to mildew is much more likely to be governed by the thickness or thinness of the cuticle on the leaves and flowers.

Root-rot

The rot referred to attacks the stool or crown, not the fibrous roots. 'Blackrot' is a misnomer; the rot experienced in Great Britain is not the fatal black rot commonly experienced in the U.S.A. but a natural collapse of the organic tissues sometimes due to old age in the plant itself, sometimes due to eelworm attack, and always capable of being accelerated either by stagnant water lying over winter in the cut-down stems or by predatory pests harboured in them. As regards the collapse of plant tissues (see Fig. 38e) the dark varieties are often more prone to it than others. My own observation is that there is considerable variation in the hardness of delphinium stools and that those of the dark varieties are often softer and more fleshy, therefore more prone to rot or collapse of tissues. This in turn may well be due to soil conditions and especially, again, the degree of acidity or alkalinity.

I feel myself that good cultivation, good drainage, and sensible feeding will go a long way towards making plants more resistant. Too much nitrogenous manure gives too lush a growth, which in

132

47. Cucumber mosaic virus

turn must mean softer crowns and increased winter vulnerability.
A good baking of the crown in summer must be specially beneficial on the heavier and wetter soils, and will give firmer and
healthier cuttings the following spring.

It must always be remembered, in other words, that these plants
are the hybrids of generations of hybrids and that they are living
in 'softer' conditions than their mountain forebears.

Virus

The Cucumber Mosaic Virus is the only virus known to attack
the delphinium in Great Britain. It has a stunting effect upon a
plant but is commonly evidenced by the narrowing and elonga-
tion of the leaf segments, coupled with extensive marbling of the
leaf-colour, as in Fig. 47. Experience shows that the susceptibility
of a plant to the virus is seed-borne, not soil-borne, and that it is
often recessive. Nevertheless it is usual to dig up and destroy a
plant so affected, merely because there is no cure. Frequently a
single stem is effected on a plant with several healthy stems; I
have, in these cases, experimented with the cutting off of the
particular crown from which the stem emanates, leaving the rest
of the plant, and have found this successful next season. I have
also sown seed from the good stems remaining and found the
seedlings healthy in the first generation. Yet none of this is really

133

conclusive and large-scale experiments alone can provide diagnosis and solution. Meanwhile, destruction is best, and if a knife is used on an infected plant it should be properly sterilized before being used again.

Fasciation

This is neither a disease nor a pest, but is conveniently mentioned here as an affliction to which an odd plant is sometimes prone and to which overfeeding can contribute. Whenever you observe distorted growth, flattening of stems, bunching of florets into a club-headed monstrosity, as seen in Fig. 48a, or a substitution of whiskery leaves for laterals as in Fig. 48b, then that is fasciation. When false springs occur, followed by a return of winter and then by an April drought, with the plants beset perhaps by cold wind, the steady process by which the root hairs take in nourishment and pass it upwards by means of the plant cells suffers constant interruption, and it is really not to be wondered at if the complex mechanism of plant life suffers. But it is no more than that and the same plants, given normal weather and anything like normal steadiness of growth next season, will flower perfectly. Only in the odd event of a plant repeating it annually should it be scrapped.

The term fasciation has its root in the Latin *fascis*, meaning a bunch or bundle, and more familiar in the plural *fasces*, signifying the bundle of rods, with protruding axe, carried by the lictors of ancient Rome.

General

For the successful cultivation of the delphinium for all garden purposes and up to good standard, the importance of virus, root-rot, mildew, and attacks by caterpillars should be kept in proper proportion. None of these is of first-rate importance in the cultivation of the plant; the incidence is so small and the breeding of plants and seed is in such very capable hands. The only pest to which all gardeners must pay attention is the slug, in four forms, viz. Grey Field, Black Field, Large Black, and Keeled. All enjoy eating the tender parts of the delphinium if given the opportunity. The smaller, keeled slug does most of the under-

48a. Fasciation

48b. Fasciation manifests itself in the absence of laterals and the extra growth of 2 ft of whiskered stem

ground damage in winter, the grey or pink-grey slug goes deep down and lays its eggs in the soil around the stool and its tiny progeny, when only a half-inch at extension, can eat the tips of the embryo and dormant 'eyes' and are fully capable of slithering up the stem even 2 ft or 3 ft until they find something tender enough for them to eat. Those very large black slugs and brown slugs, rather like the large garden snail, are not really delphinium-minded, but when the shoots are 2 ins.–3 ins. high these pests simply eat them completely off, if they find them in the way during their wanderings.

Unfortunately the succulent shoots do not have the lethal effect of the ground-up seed (see Chapter 1), but the contact-killer properly and systematically used offers a full solution.

8 · Introduction of a new plant

The story is told of an amateur who proposed cutting some spikes to put up for judging and award. Investigation showed that the plant was a seedling with three spikes, no cuttings had been taken or divisions made, and the grower had no knowledge whatsoever of any of the named plants. He was wrong on every count as the rest of this chapter should show.

Raising from seed, breeding, building up selected stocks and knowledge of the plant to the point where a stock can be justifiably named, and with some hope of success – all these things are necessary and satisfactory, but for the amateur there is no true and complete satisfaction unless fellow-gardeners are able to share his pleasure in the particular plant. For the professional this is the art of living and the climax of a job well done; for the amateur it is the finishing touch which hallmarks the hobby which is so dear to his heart. The ultimate satisfaction in breeding surely lies in seeing your handiwork shown up and down the country and grown by anyone who wishes. For the amateur breeder or raiser it is possible to gain Awards of Merit without the plants themselves ever being put into commerce; to achieve this latter the plant must be of such a high standard that the specialist nurserymen, and others who keep their collections up to date, feel like buying it.

For an amateur to select, build up and name a new plant, and contrive to get it distributed, is a long-drawn-out affair indeed.

Selection of Seedlings and Building up

Study of this book and of its illustrations will help to give the raiser of delphiniums an idea of what is wanted. Of more value than anything is his knowledge of existing plants, for if he does not know them well he cannot reasonably select varieties which are an improvement. To know delphiniums well enough will take years of study during which the raiser is growing his seedlings from selfed seed and from hand-pollinated crosses. The time comes when he makes selections, of which he commences to take cuttings.

When he has a stock of four or five good plants of a variety, it is always possible to send a plant or two to a specialist nursery for trial. If the plant is a good 'doer' and desirable, a sale may be effected outright or on a basis of an agreed royalty on future sales if any result.

In either event, apart from naming the plant, the raiser has no more work to do as the specialist is going to do it for him. Failing such an early sale, the raiser will lift his stock to thirty or forty plants. During this two- or three-year process it will become evident whether the plant really is as good as at first thought. If it is still considered desirable, it is then safe to name the plant by registering it with the Secretary of the Royal Horticultural Society. Certainly it is undesirable to name it with a small stock of two or three as they might be lost in a bad winter.

If after naming it is decided to sell at that point it is a matter of approaching the right nurseryman to give the plant a trial, but if confidence in the plant is sufficient the raiser should try to show the plant by taking cut spikes to flower shows, and especially by putting up the minimum of three specimens required for award purposes and for selection for garden trial at Wisley. The physical side of this problem – viz. the cutting, transporting, and staging of the spikes – is dealt with in Chapter 12.

Joint Delphinium Committee

Our plant is fortunate not only in that it has attracted front-rank breeders for over one hundred years, but also in that the merit of their work was speedily recognized by the Royal Horticultural Society. At their Wisley Gardens this Society held its first full-scale trial of delphiniums as long ago as 1916–17, with as many as 230 stocks. This trial was renewed again after the war in 1925 and has been a permanency ever since, being judged by Floral A Committee until 1932, whereafter a joint committee composed of the Royal Horticultural Society and the then recently formed British Delphinium Society took this task over. It should go on record that both Charles Langdon and his son Allan Langdon have been awarded the Victoria Medal of Honour by the Royal

Horticultural Society and that a Veitch Memorial Medal was awarded to the late Frank Bishop.

The delphinium lends itself to being grown for exhibition and also to being forced in pots for such early shows as the famous Chelsea Flower Show, but the main concern here is with garden performance. The regulations of the Committee referred to indicate procedure; the standards governing the spikes themselves and their condition, as well as the points scale used for judging, are all available on application so that there is nothing, except the plant itself, to prevent the raiser from having his plant accepted for trial as a garden variety.

If it has possibilities they will be recognized and the plant will in due course be judged when in growth. It may gain an Award of Merit, Highly Commended, or, in due course, a First Class Certificate; on the other hand it may gain nothing. All will really depend upon the raiser's initial judgement; if it fails it may be because of similarity to others or inferiority in performance. It may still remain a good plant but any hopes of putting it into commerce will be destined for disappointment.

Assuming an award is gained this is a satisfactory honour for an amateur but the matter should not rest there. If other gardeners are to enjoy your plant someone must distribute it and so it has to pass a second test of acceptability in a specialist nursery. As already indicated, such a sale can be an outright sale of stock at anything from thirty to three hundred plants, or a sale on a basis of royalties on results where the raiser shares the risk with the distributor.

There is, of course, honour and satisfaction in the raising and naming of a plant which goes on to gain an award. This satisfaction is very much greater if the plant is generally exhibited and sold to the gardening public.

Plant Breeders' Rights

Such a chapter as this would be incomplete without mention of the Report on Plant Breeders' Rights presented in July 1960. The main concern of this report is the present inadequacy of the breeder's reward from the proceeds of new varieties. The unanimous recommendation of the Committee is that the breeder of a distinct variety of plant should be eligible for the grant of exclusive personal rights in his variety. The grant of such rights would enable the holder to obtain a negotiated royalty for a fixed period on all propagation for sale by other persons. In the case of the delphinium the period envisaged is as much as ten years. Such a system recognizes the value of breeding and is designed to encourage breeders to raise still further the general standard of breeding, by making it more worthwhile.

9 · Belladonnas

The plants in the belladonna section are of entirely different character and habit to the *elatum* hybrids. The florets are much more nearly related to the wild delphinium, the formation being one of single petals and long spur with the floret about $\frac{3}{4}$ in. across, the stems being very slim and wiry and the foliage generally smaller and very finely divided indeed. Total height of plants in average open sites is about 3 ft–4 ft, the perenniality is good, and flowering normally occurs twice in each season.

The first belladonna came into cultivation a century ago, but hardly any development or widening of variety has occurred in that time because they are all sterile except by freak of nature. It is generally agreed that the ancestors of this small race are the wild *elatum* with thirty-two chromosomes, *grandiflorum* with sixteen and *cheilanthum* (from Siberia) with sixteen. The belladonnas themselves have forty-eight chromosomes and the *elatum* hybrids thirty-two, hence their incompatibility, consequent sterility, and lack of progress.

A natural mutation produced a white belladonna at the Royal Moerheim Nurseries at Dedemsvaart in Holland which gained an Award of Merit in 1909 and an Award after trial in 1917. A further remarkable thing about this original and rare seedling, named *D. moerheimi*, was that it had five stems and that one of them flowered light blue. Both parts of the plant propagated true to character and the light blue became the well-known belladonna 'Capri'. These two plants, together with the Oxford blue 'Lamartine' raised by Victor Lemoine in 1903, were in the 1916–17 trial at Wisley and are still represented in the Wisley Trials by direct descent.

Cobalt-blue 'Orion' also came from Dedemsvaart in 1923, as did the only semi-double, called 'Semi-plena', of pale blue and soft rose in 1917. A good gentian-blue called 'Wendy' arrived in 1932, and in 1920 'Blue Bees', a lovely sky-blue with a white eye, came from a chance seed-setting in the garden of a Mr Gibson at Leeming Bar. Another rich blue called 'Naples' came from

49. Theodor Ruys of the Royal Moerheim Nurseries at Dedemsvaart
in Holland, breeders of 'Pink Sensation', white 'Moerheimi', and
yellow 'Golden Gown'

Thompson and Morgan of Ipswich in 1930. All the varieties mentioned are still freely available, though 'Naples' is sometimes offered as 'Azure Queen'; between them they represent the pick of the few available belladonnas with the single exception of the larger-flowered pure gentian 'Bonita' bred by Mr A. T. Knight of Clandon in 1952.

Of true belladonnas, with their branching habit and dainty foliage, only one other need be mentioned and that is 'Blue Dragonfly', a bright French blue with a very yellow-haired eye and outstandingly attractive leaves. This was a new introduction in 1942 and came from the late Mr E. W. Mooring of Witley who raised it from a cross between the dwarf 'Blue Butterfly' and an *elatum* hybrid seedling. This dwarf, by the way, is a 12-in. form of wild Siberian *grandiflorum*, seed from cultivated forms of which is usually obtainable.

There remains to relate the introduction of the only existent pink perennial delphinium, known as 'Pink Sensation', bred at the Royal Moerheim Nurseries and introduced in 1936. In form of floret like a belladonna, but in habit straight-stemmed like a miniature *elatum* hybrid, this plant owes its light rose-pink colour to a natural mutation in one plant among a large sowing of the wild orange and scarlet delphinium *nudicaule*. From the second generation from this plant four scarlet plants emerged. While they themselves proved to lack vitality the crossing of them with *elatum* hybrids produced 'Pink Sensation'. But it took the raising of about 100,000 seedlings from crosses before this plant emerged and of that number only one other, deeper 'Rose Beauty', now defunct, ever succeeded. I am indebted to Mr Theodor Ruys for this interesting information.

As you see, the true belladonnas owe their very existence to the unpredictable mutations of nature and their true habit is sterile. There is therefore so little hope of improvement that no breeding work is being attempted upon them. It seems possible that they will in a few years be ousted by a new race of bushy plants from Connecticut, U.S.A., developed by Edward Steichen. These have the great advantage of being fertile seed-bearers with the single florets widely open and enlarged, and it is interesting to record that blood of selected forms of the wild delphinium *cheilanthum*, one of the dwarfing forebears of the belladonnas, has been bred into these. More information about this seed strain from the U.S.A. will be found in Chapter 14.

Also small in stature, from 1 ft to 3 ft 6 ins. in fact, are the West of the Rockies strain, bred by A. A. Samuelson of Pullman, Washington, by intercrossing *D. nudicaule*, *D. cardinale*, *D. hanseni*, *D. menziesii* and other Western American species. Seed from this strain of tuberous-rooted plants, flowering yellow, apricot, pink, scarlet, crimson, and purple, has been enjoyed by the members of the Delphinium Society but is not as yet freely in commerce. The florets are larger than belladonnas, and nearly all are single and long-spurred. Stems are wiry, foliage is finely divided and the plants themselves are perennial only in favoured warm localities or in expert hands.

10 · Wild delphiniums

Several hundred wild delphiniums exist the world over. They vary in height from a mere 6 ins. to 6 ft, they include all the shades of blue, violet, white, yellow, orange, and scarlet, they even have a fragrant scent in a few cases, and in reading about them it is easy to find oneself wishing they could all be grown in British gardens, they sound so attractive; they are in fact one of the few genera affording the three primary colours in the wild. However, though found in countries as widely separated as China, India, Africa, and Western America they invariably grow in mountainous country in almost identical conditions, sun and good drainage followed by a winter blanket of snow, and so only a very few of them can be seriously considered from a garden point of view. Furthermore, except for botanists and plant-collectors, seed in most cases cannot be procured.

Of those worth growing in the average garden and of which seed is quite easily obtained I list the following six main species:

D. tatsienense – a really worthwhile plant with rich blue, long spurred flowers loosely held on a much-branched 18-in. plant with finely divided dark green leaves, flowering June–July and best grown annually from seed. (Western China.)

D. grandiflorum – the Butterfly seed strain from selected plants, is very attractive as an annual. There are light blue, deep blue, lavender, and white forms available from seed, flowering bushily at 18 ins. in June–July from seed sown February–March. (Western N. America and Siberia.)

D. cashmirianum – this one has larger flowers, with short, fat spurs, is deep blue with touches of purple, and opens in July–August. (Himalayas.)

D. vestitum – the true form of this flowers in August and early September at 4 ft–5 ft, and has attractive florets of intense violet. It comes from the Himalayas, and the stems are slender and well clothed.

D.nudicaule – though not hardy in England this Western American species is so easily grown from seed that it should not be missed by anyone. It is never more than 12 ins.–18 ins. in height, has strong stems bearing long-spurred half-open flowers of bright vermilion scarlet, with an orange and a chamois-pink form also available. It flowers the same season as sown, and for a long period, often from June to August.

D.cardinale – the flowers of this 3-ft plant from Western America are fully open and are of the richest scarlet, borne on wiry stems in July–August. Not perennial in England. As in the case of *D.nudicaule* this plant is tuberous-rooted and likes a warm and well-drained site.

All the above are very well worth growing.

Lastly, for those who are keen enough I will throw out the challenge of six species, seed of which will be hard to come by, but which are very choice indeed:

D.brunonianum – a dwarf species from screes and high altitudes of the Himalayas. It seldom exceeds 8 ins. in height and has three or four quite large pale blue or pale mauve balloon-shaped flowers heavily veined with darker blue, hairy on the margins of the petals, with dark centres and short spurs. This plant is said to have a strong odour of musk. The leaves are deeply dissected. Probably best grown as an alpine house plant.

D.leroyi – this unusual plant grows well in Cornwall, sets seed well, and is perennial. It comes from the slopes of Mt Kilimanjaro at 4,000–6,000 ft, and is allied to *D.wellbyi* from Abyssinia. It has the delicious scent of the narcissus, flowers pale blue, mauve, off-white, and white. The florets are held closely on 2-ft branches from the main stem and in the genial climate of Cornwall the stem keeps throwing fresh branches for long periods.

D.likiangense – this plant comes from the Yunnan province of China and is about 12 ins.–15 ins. in height. Its finely divided foliage throws the erect stem up above it and on it are from three to five florets of the clearest blue imaginable. *D.likiangense* is said to be fragrant and the gem of the species.

D. macrocentron – an exciting plant from the higher grassland zones of Mt Kenya and Mt Elgon in East Africa. The comparatively large flowers are a most brilliant shade of electric greenish-blue and are borne on short stems up to 2 ft. The flowers are slightly drooping in habit. Unfortunately, like other plants from the equatorial mountains of Africa, it is usually not very long-lived in this country and should be frequently renewed from seed whenever possible. Its hardiness is also doubtful.

D. wellbyi – a small plant not often over 2 ft with short spikes of attractive, China-blue flowers about 2½ ins. across. This species comes from the highlands of Abyssinia and is hardy in the more protected gardens of the south west but in other places is best treated as a cool-greenhouse plant. It is perennial and, though seldom long-lived in this country, is quite easily raised from seed.

D. zalil – in British sunshine this desirable plant will flower pale primrose-yellow but the tuberous roots will not be perennial except in very favoured warm spots with light soil. Its native habitat is the valleys of the Gilran province of Afghanistan and Eastern Persia. It flowers at a height of 3 ft and holds its 1½-in. florets on short pedicels on erect stems (see Fig. 50).

50. The sun of 1959 suited *D. zalil* despite the cold and heavy soil in
    C. R. Broan's Cheam garden

11 · Delphiniums in the house

We have now reached an era when flowers in the house matter more than ever before. The arrangement of flowers is a world vogue and an important social asset. The hardening off of the various genera has been very carefully studied and the correct methods are becoming common knowledge. In the case of delphiniums, however, very few people seem to know how to harden them off or how to use them to full advantage. The plant still has in fact an entirely undeserved reputation as a 'messy' subject which speedily becomes a nuisance in the house.

Yet it is perfectly simple to ensure that spikes, or lateral branches or even single florets, last well for a minimum of three days in ordinary household conditions, and four is quite common. In the months of June and July temperatures run high and few flowers last any longer when cut.

The first essential is to choose spikes which are completely fresh. When one contemplates a large arrangement, as in Fig. 52, the condition of the spike speaks for itself. An individual spike in full colour and prime condition is shown in Fig. 57. Now these spikes have anything from 2 ft to 3 ft 6 ins. of bloom on them and are ideal for creating effect in large halls, on pedestals, and in fire-places. They can also be particularly useful in churches and at receptions where lofty arrangements are necessary to create visible effect. If they are to be kept fresh and durable it is vital to ensure that the entire drinking system of each spike is fully charged with water before being placed in the arrangement.

To this end it is best to have deep water-containers some 2 ft tall, with heavy bases, and to place them in a cool garage or cellar. Next, cut the spikes with a sharp knife or secateurs and snip off all foliage and laterals. Place the spikes in the deep water overnight, cutting a couple of inches off each butt *underneath the water*, as in Fig. 58a. This cut below water is necessary to prevent any air-lock forming in the fleshy rim through which the water is passed upwards into all the extremities. If an air-lock forms a

51. Florets of sky-blue, 3 ins. across, and on fine long pedicels, accompanied by pink *Escallonia*, the whole in a claret coloured glass container. A delightful and artistic arrangement by Mrs Cecil Pope of Dorchester

spike can stay in water for a whole day or more but will not drink at all.

By the means indicated the whole cell system is saturated with water, even the little pedicels which hold the florets on the main stem, and the arranger can proceed to use these spikes in large arrangements, or the florets in small ones, without fear. Should the laterals in bud or in bloom be required exactly the same procedure should be followed.

For bold effects, in its unrivalled and cool colours, the delphinium is supreme. The arching sprays formed by smaller seedling spikes or by the side-branches from the main spikes are all that could be desired for giving height and width to order, coupled with grace and elegance. As background to or framework of an arrangement of any size it is hard to improve upon the delphinium. And its florets and small sprigs in bud or in flower, afford great scope for the unusual (see Figs. 51 and 53). The delphinium is also specially suited to the modern practice of stripping the stems of side growths and leaves and using the bloom only, with contrasting foliage such as Onopordon, globe artichoke, and so on. The removal of foliage and laterals is helpful in keeping the blooms fresh.

52. A majestic show-piece, eminently suited to a hearth or to a deep window-sill. A simple composition of exhibition spikes of light blue offset by copper beech foliage. Designed by Mrs Cecil Pope

53. Mrs H. Winbourne of Esher effectively demonstrates the suitability of the delphinium to the Japanese style

150

54. Mrs N. Gibson of Cobham has a talent for pedestals, for which the
large spikes are particularly suited

12 · Delphiniums for exhibition

Few can bring themselves to cut delphinium spikes in bloom and most of those who would like to exhibit their blooms jib at the thought of transporting them to shows. None can deny, however, that the plant is a noble and impressive sight; it would indeed be hard to find a flower which lends itself to exhibition so well, so the problems of growing and transporting have to be tackled.

For local flower shows and even for the Delphinium Society's London Show, spikes of sufficient merit can frequently be found among the plants which decorate the herbaceous border. Winning spikes have been known to be cut from such plants eight and nine years of age, so no one need feel discouraged. Nevertheless, there are better methods of growing and selection for show purposes.

The very best results are to be expected from plants, struck from cuttings, when flowering in their first or second season after striking. Such plants should be planted, in rows 3 ft – 4 ft apart with 2 ft – 2 ft 6 ins. between individual plants, in really well-prepared ground. At thinning time they should be reduced to from one to three stems according to vigour, and they should be fed with a liquid feed once every five or six days, after attaining a height of 2 ft and up to when the buds on the spikes, fully stretched, show colour. The most important part of this feed is really the water content and two gallons per plant per five days of this alone will help to ensure that the spike is evenly formed and the stem true and tapering.

For intensity of colour, potash is essential and the best form is sulphate of potash, half an ounce of which per two gallons per plant per five days is ample and ideal. For hardness of stem and to promote root growth phosphates are required; for the quick action necessary superphosphate of lime is suitable, in the same proportions as the sulphate of potash. Many growers of exhibition blooms believe in nitrogen, thus insisting on the balanced feed which is usual for plant growth. If required, nitro-chalk or sulphate of ammonia provide nitrogen readily. Personally I prefer to rely on the preparation of the ground in which the delphiniums are planted; if well manured it should be sufficient in itself and it must be remembered that if the nitrogen is overdone the growth will be lush and soft, and therefore very liable to damage from bad weather.

To sum up, I favour a five-day solution of $\frac{1}{2}$ oz. each of potash and phosphates to two gallons of water per plant. In cases where the heavy work of liquid feeding cannot be undertaken a second-best method is to put on a 4-in. or 5-in. surface-mulch when the plants are 2 ft high and to use sprinkler or sprayline to dissolve and wash in the feed. Such mulch can be of cow manure, pig manure, guano, or merely compost treated with concentrated liquid seaweed.

The ground should be kept hoed with a fine 2-in. tilth on top. The plants should be watched daily, and kept slug-free and caterpillar-free. Extra precautions should be taken where tying is concerned and in some windier sites light 'carnation tips' may even have to be tied with raffia right up through the spike itself.

For show purposes the rules demand that a spike should be furnished with three laterals. Most plants throw many more than this per spike and one of the daily attentions will be to rub out the young unwanted laterals with finger and thumb when an inch or so long. It is usual to leave the three lowest and to remove those higher up because they impede the judges' view of the spike.

A word or two about timing will be apt. To meet the needs of a specified show date appropriate choice of early, mid-season, or late flowering varieties should be made, and to help combat the vagaries of nature it is very useful to duplicate the planting, one in a border facing south and the other in a border facing north. By these means you should have the same variety coming into bloom over a period of fourteen days, enough to meet most changing situations.

On the subject of selection of spikes for exhibition, freshness is the first consideration. There must be no gaps amongst the florets and seed pods must not be visible – scrutiny of Figs. 56 and 57 will help. The spike should be as fully open as possible but never at the expense of the basal florets, the eye petals and main petals of which must be complete.

55a. At this stage, with the embryo spikes just thrusting clear of the foliage, it takes about twenty-eight days for the spikes to develop

55b. The same, four weeks later, with several spikes in good show condition

154

56a. A well-formed spike with one bad blemish at the base

56b. This spike might conceivably start dropping at the base before the
judges saw it

Formation of spike should be pleasing to the eye and well-proportioned. This implies perfect placing of florets and symmetry of spike. Each floret should be well displayed, and at the same time the stem itself should not be visible. Subject to quality and proportion, the longer the spike the better. The colour should be clear, decisive, and desirable, and the formation of florets should be semi-double or double rather than single. The only other point worth considering is the choice between a pyramidal form and a columnar form. This really comes under the heading of proportion because if a columnar or narrow spike is 3 ft 6 ins. or 4 ft long the base appears to be too narrow for the height, and on these grounds the pyramidal or wide-based spike is preferable. Human nature being what it is, one might advance the generalization that broad pyramidal spikes such as 'Guy Langdon' and 'Royal Marine' (see Figs. 17 and 71) are more likely to impress the judges. Good examples of columnar spikes such as 'Swanlake' and 'Savrola' can be seen in Figs. 13 and 72.

But mere size does not mean everything. Freshness and proportion are prime virtues, quite easily attainable in a smaller spike, and it is an extremely difficult thing to find a giant spike which has perfect show formation.

The hardening of the blooms has been dealt with in the preceding chapter. The only word that needs to be added is that cutting in the case of show flowers should take place either one or two days before the show. If staging is to be done on the day of the show cut the day before, if on the day before the show then cut two days before. This is necessary normally for reasons of hardening but also to ensure that the blooms are dry before being packed.

The great thing to remember about packing delphiniums is that each spike must be kept separate to prevent tangling of florets and spurs. It is best to roll each spike in large-size tissue paper; thereafter up to six or seven spikes may be held by the butt and nursed by hand for a short distance. Alternatively they may be laid on a flat car floor or placed in cardboard or wooden flower boxes; such methods are successfully used for distances of up to 150 miles by car or train.

But by far the best method is to carry the cut blooms in water

57. A perfect state of development for cutting, hardening overnight, packing, and transporting to the show

in the original hardening receptacles. This can be done in the arms or in a small van or estate wagon, according to scale and distance. Keep all the spikes upright by padding the neck of the container with sacking or newspaper, and all should be well.

By either method the spikes are fully charged with water and will stand transit well, and it only remains to stage them in the containers provided. Fill the containers with water, cut the spike afresh *under water* as in Fig. 58b, and wedge upright with sections of stem or other material.

As regards the plants, ideally they should never be completely shorn of stems but if this has to happen they should be heavily watered and induced to send up shoots again, thinned to one stem, flowered, and seeded. They should be rested from cutting the following season, whereafter they will be back in good health. Perfectionists would throw them away, but it is not necessary as they have many years of garden value still. However, plants for exhibition should normally be renewed from cuttings every third year to ensure vigour and quality and at the same time to keep them to manageable proportions.

157

58a. If your spikes are to travel well and hold in fresh condition at the show, each must be cut under water overnight to ensure that it drinks its fill

58b. The underwater cut should be repeated when staging, otherwise an air-lock may form and the spike will not drink at all at the show

158

13 · Worthwhile named varieties

To the average gardener for whom this book is mainly written, the principal factors which go to make one delphinium different from another to an important degree are as follows – colour and shape of petals; colour, shape, and size of bee; height; season of flowering; size of florets and spike. There are small florets and large florets; spikes 2 ft long and 4 ft long; narrow spikes and broad spikes; insignificant bees and large conspicuous bees; pointed petals and rounded petals; flat florets and frilled florets. With all these ingredients the possible permutations, each producing an entirely different-looking plant, are endless. Constitution is, of course, a *sine qua non* in a good plant and all my selections are good 'doers'. There remains the important matter of season of flowering.

Now delphiniums do not all flower at the same time. A great many are so widely separated in season that they are never seen in bloom together, and I have found it practical to divide my choice into five distinct but overlapping groups – early, early to mid-season, mid-season, mid-season to late, and late. As regards colour I have used eleven main divisions in order to help to differentiate as much as possible, and I have included the very latest as well as impending introductions in order to ensure an up-to-date list with a lengthy future in front of it. Each variety has been placed according to its main colour, that is, the colour of the front or inner petals and not the colour of its back petals, of which the tips only are visible.

In cultivation today there must be fully 250 varieties but many of these are obsolete and others are rapidly becoming so. The remainder have been reduced to a manageable sixty-six to make what I believe to be the best representative collection possible, and I have marked with an asterisk thirty plants which are considered to be quite outstanding in quality.

Under the heading 'Awards' the following abbreviations have been used: A.M.-E. for Award of Merit as a flower for exhibition; A.M.-G. for Award of Merit as a garden flower; A.M.-Trials for

Award of Merit after trials; F.C.C. for First Class Certificate, and H.C. for Highly Commended.

1. WHITE AND NEAR-WHITE

Early

'Swanlake'

Height: 5 ft 6 ins. *Length of Spike:* 3 ft *Diameter of Floret:* 3 ins.
Raiser, Introducer: Bishop, Bakers *Year of Introduction:* 1954

There is as yet no pure white in this section. 'Swanlake' has a narrow or columnar spike, a steel-grey tinge in the unopened buds and a pinkish tone in the petals on opening. The eye is jet-black, of medium size and flat.

Early to Mid-Season

'Snow White'

Height: 5 ft 6 ins. *Length of Spike:* 2 ft 6 ins. *Diameter of Floret:* 3 ins.
Raiser, Introducer: Blackmore & Langdon *Year of Introduction:* 1959

A pure white with a narrowly pyramidal spike. The florets are rounded and the eye is flat

'White Nylon'

Height: 5 ft *Length of Spike:* 2 ft 6 ins. *Diameter of Floret:* 2½ ins.
Raiser, Introducer: A. E. J. B. Kidney, R. C. Parrett *Year of Introduction:* 1961

Pure white, pyramidal spike, with frilled and pointed petals and a pleasant vanilla-like scent. The medium-sized eye is an attractive creamy-yellow.

Mid-Season

* 'Sunday Express'

Height: 5 ft *Length of Spike:* 3 ft 6 ins. *Diameter of Floret:* 2½ ins.
Raiser, Introducer: R. C. Parrett, Bakers *Awards:* A.M.-E., 1959; H.C., 1961

Pure white and pyramidal with a notably hard, slender, and straight stem, and perfect placement. The rounded florets commence only 18 ins. from the ground; the large eye is white and green and yellow in an attractive claw-like cluster. The plant is very sturdy, needing only a single tie.

59. 'Sunday Express', which gained a 1959 A.M. for Exhibition, is a grand, straight-growing garden plant. Like its stable companion, 'Daily Express', it was a chance seedling from the Bishop strain

Mid-Season to Late

'Janice'

Height: 3 ft 6 ins.   *Length of Spike:* 2 ft 6 ins.   *Diameter of Floret:* 3 ins.
Raiser, Introducer: Bishop, Bakers   *Year of Introduction:* 1952

An extremely sturdy plant with a heavy spike; only one tie necessary. Purest of whites with a medium-sized white and rounded eye.

Late

'Antarctic'

Height: 4 ft 6 ins.   *Length of Spike:* 2 ft 6 ins.   *Diameter of Floret:* 3 ins.
Raiser, Introducer: Bishop, Bakers   *Year of Introduction:* 1958

A particularly attractive plant with glacial blue-grey shadings in the white, rounded, and slightly cupped florets. The eye is creamy white and flat and the spikes are solid, well-formed, and well tapered. A unique plant which should be particularly popular for flower arrangement.

'Purity'

Height: 4 ft   *Length of Spike:* 2 ft   *Diameter of Floret:* 3 ins
Raiser, Introducer: Bishop, Bakers   *Year of Introduction:* 1961

Despite its semi-dwarfness 'Purity' has a fine pyramidal spike and is exceptionally vigorous. The eye is creamy white with yellow hairs, and formally rounded, as are the florets also.

Of the above seven white varieties only one has a black eye, and two are not pure white. All have the virtue of great substance in the petal so that the bottom florets stay on until long after the topmost ones are out.

2 . PURE LIGHT BLUE

Early

'Charles F. Langdon'

Height: 6 ft 6 ins.–7 ft 6 ins.   *Length of Spike:* 4 ft   *Diameter of Floret:* 3 ins.
Raiser, Introducer: Blackmore & Langdon   *Year of Introduction:* 1948
Awards: A.M.-Trials, 1948; F.C.C. 1949

A bright sky-blue, a shade deeper than the others in this group. The florets are flat and rounded, with a large black and gold eye. The spike is broad-based. Almost immune to mildew. Stems a little fleshy and prone to breakage.

60. The graceful tapering spikes of 'Sea Mist', a lovely glistening light blue with a sheen of mother-of-pearl

Early to Mid-Season

* 'Sonata'

Height: 6 ft–6 ft 6 ins. *Length of Spike:* 3 ft *Diameter of Floret:* 2½ ins.
Raiser, Introducer: Blackmore & Langdon *Year of Introduction:* 1951
Awards: A.M.-Trials, 1958

A graceful pyramidal spike of bright sky-blue, tapering finely and very mildew-resistant. The florets have pointed petals and a small, creamy-white eye.

'Caprice'

Height: 4 ft 6 ins. *Length of Spike:* 2 ft 6 ins. *Diameter of Floret:* 2½ ins.
Raiser, Introducer: Bishop, Bakers *Year of Introduction:* 1955

This plant stands well in bad weather. The florets have pointed petals and a large white eye, and the colour is a fine sky-blue self.

Mid-Season

* 'Sea Mist'

Height: 5 ft *Length of Spike:* 2 ft 6 ins. *Diameter of Floret:* 3 ins.
Raiser, Introducer: Blackmore & Langdon *Year of Introduction:* 1955
Awards: A.M.-E., 1957; H.C., 1959; A.M.-G., 1960; F.C.C., 1961

The petals are round and formal, sometimes a little cupped; eye white and inconspicuous. The overall colour effect is a delicate shade of light blue with an overlay of mother-of-pearl. A pyramidal and beautifully tapered spike; very resistant to mildew.

* 'Daily Express'

Height: 5 ft–5 ft 6 ins. *Length of Spike:* 3 ft–3 ft 6 ins. *Diameter of Floret:* 3 ins.–3½ ins.
Raiser, Introducer: R. C. Parrett, Toynbees *Year of Introduction:* 1949
Awards: A.M.-Trials, 1955; A.M.-E., 1955; F.C.C., 1961

The florets are of a very bright and pure sky-blue with slight frilling at the edges. They are exceptionally long-lasting and the plant is particularly long-living and vigorous; mildew-resistance good. The dark brown eye is a little untidy in appearance and the stems can come a little coarse in wet seasons.

* 'Blue Jade'

Height: 4 ft–4 ft 6 ins. *Length of Spike:* 2 ft–2 ft 6 ins. *Diameter of Floret:* 2½ ins.
Raiser, Introducer: Blackmore & Langdon *Year of Introduction:* 1958
Awards: A.M.-G., 1960

A pure soft sky-blue of a very desirable height, with a compact and flat light brown eye, touched white. The petals are broad but slightly pointed. A plant representing a very big advance in breeding and possessing all the virtues; the spikes are pyramidal and beautifully tapered.

61. The variety 'Daily Express', growing at Wisley, and which has gained the A.M. both for Garden and Exhibition. A chance seedling from seed of the Bishop strain

This is a very strong trio of plants in one of the delphinium's most attractive colours. Each differs from its companions in the section and each is quite outstanding.

Mid-Season to Late

'Skylark'

Height: 5 ft *Length of Spike:* 2 ft 6 ins. *Diameter of Floret:* 2½ ins.
Raiser, Introducer: Bishop, Bakers *Year of Introduction:* 1958

A pyramidal spike of Cambridge blue, very pure indeed and gracefully tapered. The petals are flat and rounded and the eye is a neat one, white and protruding.

'Nora O'Fallon'

Height: 5 ft 6 ins. *Length of Spike:* 2 ft 6 ins. *Diameter of Floret:* 2½ ins.
Raiser, Introducer: Bishop, Bakers *Year of Introduction:* 1956

Lovely, pure, silvery blue with a conspicuous large and flat black eye. The florets are flat and rounded and of great substance and texture. The columnar spike is notable for the perfect symmetry of its build. Mildew-resistance good.

'Pageboy'

Height: 3 ft 6 ins. *Length of Spike:* 1 ft 6 ins.–2 ft *Diameter of Floret:* 2 ins.
Raiser, Introducer: Blackmore & Langdon *Year of Introduction:* 1959
Award: A. M.-G., 1961

Consistently rich sky-blue, with a contrasting and conspicuous black eye, striped blue; florets often slightly cupped. A columnar spike, beautifully tapered; very resistant to mildew.

Late

* 'Betty Hay'

Height: 5 ft 6 ins. *Length of Spike:* 3 ft *Diameter of Floret:* 2½ ins.
Raiser, Introducer: Blackmore & Langdon *Year of Introduction:* 1957
Awards: A.M.-Trials, 1958; F.C.C., 1961

The whole of the petals, back and front, is a soft sky-blue of the utmost purity. The petals are pointed and the spike tapers to perfection, with an unusually large number of florets, arranged pyramidally. A very valuable plant for lateness and for purity of colour; eye creamy-white, small, and compact.

62. Our photographer, height 5 ft 8 ins., demonstrated the virtues of a lovely light blue called 'Blue Jade'

3 . LIGHT BLUE WITH ROSY FLUSH

Early

'Lady Eleanor'

Height: 6 ft–7 ft *Length of Spike:* 3 ft *Diameter of Floret:* 2¾ ins.
Raiser, Introducer: Blackmore & Langdon *Year of Introduction:* 1930
Awards: A.M.-E., 1931; A.M.-Trials, 1933; F.C.C., 1935

A soft sky-blue, flushed silvery mauve, the florets are fully double and eyeless. The spike is columnar. Although now a veteran this plant is unique and popular.

Early to Mid-Season

* 'Arcadia'

Height: 6 ft *Length of Spike:* 3 ft *Diameter of Floret:* 3½ ins.
Raiser, Introducer: Blackmore & Langdon *Year of Introduction:* 1954

The sky-blue petals are strongly flushed with rosy-mauve and become almost pure blue as they mature. The eye is creamy white, flat, and unobtrusive. The spikes are broad and well-built, and a strong clump, with spikes in various stages of development, creates pleasing contrasts between rosy mauve and blue. Mildew-resistance good.

'Blue Dawn'

Height: 5 ft–5 ft 6 ins. *Length of Spike:* 2 ft 6 ins.–3 ft *Diameter of Floret:* 2½ ins.–3 ins. *Raiser, Introducer:* Blackmore & Langdon *Year of Introduction:* 1957
Award: H.C., 1960

A fine example of the value of the central 'bee' – in this case, small, compact, and black and gold. In all other respects this plant has similarity to 'Arcadia', having the same attractive habit of ageing gracefully from rosy-mauve to blue. The black eye in this case, white in the other, create two entirely different effects.

'Mazurka'

Height: 5 ft 6 ins. *Length of Spike:* 2 ft 6 ins. *Diameter of Floret:* 3 ins.
Raiser, Introducer: Blackmore & Langdon *Year of Introduction:* 1954
Award: H.C., 1960

The spike is not quite so broad as 'Blue Dawn', but is still pyramidal and tapers well. The inner petals of sky-blue are evenly flushed pale rosy mauve and remain so; the outers are sky-blue. The eye is very large, flat and black with blue stripes, and creates yet another picture with the same artists' materials.

Mid-Season

'Anona'

Height: 4 ft 6 ins.–5 ft *Length of Spike:* 3 ft *Diameter of Floret:* 3¾ ins.
Raiser, Introducer: Blackmore & Langdon *Year of Introduction:* 1952
Awards: A.M.-E., 1952; A.M.-Trials, 1955; F.C.C., 1956

In many ways a slightly larger version of 'Sea Mist' but with more pinky mauve; not so broad in the spike and not quite so elegant and well-tapered. The individual florets are perfect, being large, flat, and rounded with a neat creamy-white eye.

4 . LIGHT MAUVE FLUSHED SKY-BLUE

Early

'Jennifer Langdon'

Height: 5 ft–5 ft 6 ins. *Length of Spike:* 2 ft 6 ins.–3 ft *Diameter of Floret:* 3½ in
Raiser, Introducer: Blackmore & Langdon *Year of Introduction:* 1949
Award: A.M.-E., 1946

A pale pinky mauve with sky-blue tips on the outers, petals round, flat and of fine substance and texture. The florets hold in phenomenal fashion and the plant is almost immune to mildew; eye small and dark brown.

Early to Mid-Season

* 'Lola'

Height: 6 ft–6 ft 6 ins. *Length of Spike:* 3 ft *Diameter of Floret:* 3½ ins.
Raiser, Introducer: Blackmore & Langdon *Year of Introduction:* 1958
Awards: A.M.-E., 1954; H.C., 1956; A.M.-Trials, 1958

A pale pinky mauve with a slight flush of very pale sky-blue on rounded petals; eye cream-coloured and protruding. A massive and pyramidal spike.

* 'Silver Moon'

Height: 6 ft *Length of Spike:* 3 ft *Diameter of Floret:* 3½ ins.
Raiser, Introducer: Blackmore & Langdon *Year of Introduction:* 1953
Awards: A.M.-E., 1954; A.M.-Trials, 1955; F.C.C., 1956

The inner, or front, petals are the palest mauve with a silvery sheen upon them; the visible tips of the back petals are a light shade of sky-blue. The petals are very flat and rounded and the eye is creamy white with yellow hairs. The pedicels holding the florets are very long at the base of the spike, giving great width, and the spike itself has perfect placement and is beautifully tapered. The whole plant gives out an aura of health and vigour; mildew-resistance is very good. The plant is a milestone in breeding, which has set a standard by which contemporary varieties are judged.

'Merrie England'

Height: 5 ft 6 ins. *Length of Spike:* 3 ft *Diameter of Floret:* 3 ins.
Raiser, Introducer: Bishop, Bakers *Year of Introduction:* 1954

A light shade of rosy mauve, with sky-blue tips to the back petals. Instead of a formal eye of white or brown or black, there are a few extra little petals in claw-like formation, rosy mauve in colour with splashes of creamy white. An extremely pretty floret; the spike is pyramidal and well tapered.

Mid-Season to Late

'Julia Langdon'

Height: 5 ft–5 ft 6 ins. *Length of Spike:* 2 ft 6 ins. *Diameter of Floret:* 3½ ins.
Raiser, Introducer: Blackmore & Langdon *Year of Introduction:* 1947
Awards: A.M.-Trials, 1948; F.C.C., 1961

A bright amethyst with the outers touched sky-blue, and a flat creamy-yellow eye. The florets are rounded and flat and always perfectly placed on a broadly pyramidal and well-tapered spike.

'Ringdove'

Height: 5 ft 6 ins.–6 ft *Length of Spike:* 2 ft 9 ins. *Diameter of Floret:* 3½ ins.
Raiser, Introducer: Blackmore & Langdon *Year of Introduction:* 1960
Award: A.M.-E., 1959

The inner and outer petals are rounded and flat, of a particularly lovely and distinctive pale pinky dove-grey with a silvery sheen, with good substance and texture. There is a contrasting nigger-brown eye with gold hairs; the spike is pyramidal and well-tapered. Practically immune to mildew.

'New Zealand'

Height: 5 ft 6 ins. *Length of Spike:* 3 ft 6 ins. *Diameter of Floret:* 3½ ins.–4 ins.
Raiser, Introducer: Bishop, Bakers *Year of Introduction:* 1961

A typical Commonwealth strain plant with large rounded florets and a lengthy, well-built spike. The colour is a pure lavender and the prominent eye is light brown.

63. With its lovely pastel colouring of silvery mauve, with touches of pale blue on the visible tips of the back petals, 'Silver Moon' is one of the very finest plants ever bred at Bath and has all the virtues a really good delphinium should have

64. 'Julia Langdon' is an extremely reliable plant with spikes which are invariably symmetrical, in a pleasing shade of rosy mauve

171

Late

* 'Great Scot'

Height: 6 ft *Length of Spike:* 3 ft 6 ins. *Diameter of Floret:* 3½ ins.–3¾ ins.
Raiser, Introducer: Blackmore & Langdon *Year of Introduction:* 1961
Award: A.M.-E., 1958

Very broad-based pyramidal spikes with petals of immense substance, rounded and flat. The florets are silvery pinky mauve in colour, with touches of sky-blue; eye white and flat. A plant of the highest class.

'Bridesmaid'

Height: 6 ft 6 ins.–8 ft *Length of Spike:* 4 ft–5 ft *Diameter of Floret:* 3 ins.–3¼ ins.
Raiser, Introducer: Blackmore & Langdon *Year of Introduction:* 1938
Awards: A.M.-Trials, 1945; F.C.C., 1949

Twenty-two years old, as I write, and still going strong. A very beautiful silvery mauve, with touches of very pale blue, eye creamy white. The rounded florets are on particularly long stalks, sometimes 12 ins.–15 ins. at the base, but held at a very acute angle, giving a columnar spike. An exceptionally fine garden and exhibition variety with a long history of success.

5 . HELIOTROPE

This is an entirely new colour in British named plants but is commonly found in Giant Pacific Lancelot and Round Table seedlings. The original heliotrope was 'Statuaire Rude'; the colour is referred to as light Cobalt-violet in the Horticultural Colour Chart. In its softer shades it is better known as heliotrope, and it deepens to Parma-violet. In delphiniums these colours are quite distinct from light mauves, lavenders, and amethysts.

Mid-Season

'Ceylon'

Height: 5 ft *Length of Spike:* 3 ft 6 ins. *Diameter of Floret:* 3¾ ins.
Raiser, Introduced: Bishop, Bakers *Year of Introduction:* 1959

This is a Commonwealth plant with typical large and healthy foliage and breadth of spike. A creamy-white and distinctive eye is on a floret of the palest shade of heliotrope imaginable, giving an effect verging on grey. It is a colour not to be found in any other named variety and is subtly attractive. The plant itself is a particularly good 'doer'.

65. 'Cinderella' is a very
well-habited plant,
with spikes and laterals
of particularly good
formation on a plant
3 ft 6 ins. to 4 ft in
height. The colour is a
clear heliotrope

Harmony'

Height: 4 ft 6 ins. *Length of Spike:* 2 ft 6 ins. *Diameter of Floret:* 2½ ins.
Raiser, Introducer: Bishop, Bakers *Year of Introduction:* 1961

Pure heliotrope inner petals with rich gentian tips to the back petals. Lovely colour combination, rounded florets, and a shapely spike, with a flat eye, black in colour, touched heliotrope.

Mid-Season to Late

* 'Great Britain'

Height: 5 ft *Length of Spike:* 3 ft *Diameter of Floret:* 4 ins.
Raiser, Introducer: Bishop, Bakers *Year of Introduction:* 1957
Award: A.M.-Trials, 1958

Huge Commonwealth florets of exceptional substance, a light heliotrope self with a rounded white eye. The petals are broad and bluntly pointed, forming a splendidly balanced and broadly pyramidal spike, tapering to perfection.

* 'Cinderella'

Height: 3 ft 6 ins.–4 ft *Length of Spike:* 2 ft–2 ft 6 ins. *Diameter of Floret:*
2½ ins. *Raiser, Introducer:* Bishop, Bakers *Year of Introduction:* 1954
Award: H.C., 1960

This plant is a little gem. The spikes are beautifully formed and tapered, and the laterals are notably plentiful and strong. The florets are neatly rounded, the colour being a deeper and brighter shade of heliotrope than 'Great Britain'. The eye is small and neat, light brown with heliotrope markings.

Late

* 'Canada'

Height: 5 ft *Length of Spike:* 3 ft *Diameter of Floret:* 3½ ins.–4 ins.
Raiser, Introducer: Bishop, Bakers *Year of Introduction:* 1958

The inner petals are pure pale heliotrope, with touches of sky-blue on the tips of the outers. The eye of black and heliotrope stripes is arresting and beautiful and the somewhat rounded florets are slightly frilled on the outer edges, building into a truly majestic spike of perfect formation. As with all the Commonwealth strain the plant is practically immune to mildew.

66. A single spike of rich-blue 'Cristella' which gained an Award of Merit at Wisley in 1959

175

6 . PURE MID-BLUE

Early

* 'Cristella'

Height: 5 ft–5 ft 6 ins. *Length of Spike:* 2 ft 6 ins. *Diameter of Floret:* 3 ins.
Raiser, Introducer: Blackmore & Langdon *Year of Introduction:* 1958
Awards: A.M.-Trials, 1959; F.C.C., 1961

A bright French blue of remarkable lasting powers; spikes at Wisley in the heat of 1959 were fully out to the top, yet intact at the base. A pyramidal spike, the florets flat and rounded, sometimes slightly reflexed, and the eye large and creamy white.

Mid-Season

'Blue Pearl'

Height: 4 ft–4 ft 6 ins. *Length of Spike:* 2 ft–2 ft 6 ins. *Diameter of Floret:* 2 ins.–2½ ins.
Raiser, Introducer: Bishop, Bakers *Year of Introduction:* 1954

A delightful cornflower-blue on lovely slender stems; plenty of laterals. The florets are very distinctive, being rounded and flat with a neat claw-like protruding cluster of little petals at the centre, blue striped black.

'Bebe'

Height: 4 ft *Length of Spike:* 2 ft–2 ft 3 ins. *Diameter of Floret:* 3 ins.–3½ ins.
Raiser, Introducer: Blackmore & Langdon *Year of Introduction:* 1960
Awards: A.M.-Trials, 1961; A.M.-G., 1961

A completely pure gentian with petals of great substance and a gracefully tapered pyramidal spike. An ideal plant for the windswept garden. The best of the new semi-dwarf strain from Bath, with large florets and a conspicuous flat blue-and-white striped eye.

'Star of Eve'

Height: 5 ft *Length of Spike:* 3 ft 6 ins. *Diameter of Floret:* 3 ins.
Raiser, Introducer: Bishop, Bakers *Year of Introduction:* 1957

A very pure cobalt-blue, that is, a blue a shade or so darker than French blue or gentian. The petals are flat and pointed and build into an elegant spike, often well over 4 ft, with the bottom florets only 12 ins. from the ground. The eye is white and formal.

'Maritime'

Height: 4 ft 6 ins. *Length of Spike:* 2 ft 6 ins. *Diameter of Floret:* 3½ ins.
Raiser, Introducer: Blackmore & Langdon *Year of Introduction:* 1961
Award: A.M.-G., 1960

This pure and intense mid-blue, say deep sky-blue, was the outstanding plant in the whole of the Wisley Trials in 1960.

67. 'Mollie Buchanan', a magnificent and intensely vivid gentian, one
of a new range recently introduced at Bath, which earned a
unanimous A.M. as an Exhibition variety on its first appearance at
Vincent Square .

Mid-Season to Late

'Marion'

Height: 4 ft–4 ft 6 ins. *Length of Spike:* 2 ft 6 ins. *Diameter of Floret:* 3 ins.
Raiser, Introducer: Blackmore & Langdon *Year of Introduction:* 1951
Awards: H.C., 1955; A.M.-Trials, 1956

Valuable garden plant on strong, easily staked stems. A light gentian of good substance, with a creamy-white eye with mauve markings. The florets are rounded and flat, and the spike columnar.

* 'Robin Hood'

Height: 5 ft *Length of Spike:* 3 ft *Diameter of Floret:* 3 ins.
Raiser, Introducer: Bishop, Bakers

Inner petals pure gentian, with a flat white eye, and with touches of rich violet-blue on the tips of the back petals. These are pointed, and the spikes are beautifully tapered on slender stems. A typical Bishop plant in form and colour.

Late

* 'Mollie Buchanan'

Height: 6 ft *Length of Spike:* 3 ft *Diameter of Floret:* 3 ins.
Raiser, Introducer: Blackmore & Langdon *Year of Introduction:* 1959
Award: A.M.-E., 1959

One of the best blues yet produced at Bath, this is a vivid deep gentian – a pure cobalt-blue. The petals are broad but bluntly pointed and flat, their beauty enhanced by a large flat black eye with gold hairs. The formation of the well-tapered spike is well-nigh perfect.

'Destiny'

Height: 5 ft 6 ins. *Length of Spike:* 3 ft–3 ft 6 ins. *Diameter of Floret:* 3 ins.
Raiser, Introducer: Bishop, Bakers *Year of Introduction:* 1957

A brilliant and pure French blue, or lighter gentian, with a flat white eye. The florets are flat and rounded on well-furnished and graceful spikes.

'Fidelity'

Height: 5 ft 6 ins. *Length of Spike:* 3 ft–3 ft 6 ins. *Diameter of Floret:* 3 ins.
Raiser, Introducer: Bishop, Bakers

Very well-formed columnar spikes of bright cobalt-blue, or deep gentian, with rounded and slightly cupped florets and a protruding eye of black, striped cobalt-blue.

68. 'Fidelity' is a late-flowering cobalt-blue with a black and cobalt eye

69. This is 'Greville Stevens', the brightest and purest gentian possible and promising fair to be the blue counterpart of the famous silvery mauve 'Silver Moon'. Both are plants which are going to have a very long innings

179

* 'Greville Stevens'

Height: 6 ft   *Length of Spike:* 3 ft–3 ft 3 ins.   *Diameter of Floret:* 2¾ ins.–3 ins.
Raiser, Introducer: Blackmore & Langdon   *Year of Introduction:* 1959
Awards; A.M.-E., 1959; A.M.-G., 1961

The petals are rounded and flat, of a vivid gentian of absolute purity. The spike is pyramidal, elegantly built, and finely tapering. The vigour is unequalled; this plant is the finest blue ever bred at Bath, where it is hailed as the blue counterpart of 'Silver Moon'. The brightness of the blue is emphasized by the prominent creamy-white eye, with yellow hairs.

7 . MID-BLUE WITH ROSY FLUSH

Early to Mid-Season

* 'South Seas'

Height: 6 ft–6 ft 6 ins.   *Length of Spike:* 3 ft   *Diameter of Floret:* 3 ins.–3½ ins.
Raiser, Introducer: Blackmore & Langdon   *Year of Introduction:* 1957
Award: A.M.-E., 1958

The front petals are a vivid peacock-blue with very slight rosy-indigo flush and the outer petals are peacock-blue. The florets are rounded and flat with a large blue and white protruding eye; growth is unusually strong but resistance to mildew not as good as in other varieties.

* 'Sydney'

Height: 5 ft 6 ins.   *Length of Spike:* 3 ft–3 ft 6 ins.   *Diameter of Floret:* 3½ ins.–3¾ ins.
Raiser, Introducer: Bishop, Bakers   *Year of Introduction:* 1961

A very bright French blue with a light rose flush, with the solid wide spike typical of the Commonwealth strain. The eye is conspicuous, with its blue and white stripe.

Mid-Season

'Moon Rocket'

Height: 5 ft 6 ins.   *Length of Spike:* 3 ft   *Diameter of Floret:* 3 ins.
Raiser, Introducer: Bishop, Bakers   *Year of Introduction:* 1955

A lovely mid-blue with rounded florets, forming a well-built narrowly pyramidal spike. This plant has the same attractive habit as 'Arcadia' inasmuch as the flush of rose on the immature florets contrasts pleasingly with the purer blue at maturity. The eye is formal, flat, and white in colour.

70. Brian Langdon ably demonstrates the semi-dwarf habit of 'Blue Tit', a plant which undoubtedly heralds a new delphinium era in which seed will be available to flower at heights from 3 ft to 4 ft only

8 . DARK BLUE

Early

* 'Blue Tit'

> *Height:* 3 ft 6 ins.–4 ft *Length of Spike:* 1 ft 6 ins.–2 ft *Diameter of Floret:*
> 2 ins.–2½ ins.
> *Raiser, Introducer:* Blackmore & Langdon *Year of Introduction* 1956
> *Awards:* A.M.-Trials, 1959: F.C.C., 1961

The front petals are deep royal blue touched with indigo and the tips of the back petals are royal blue. The eye is dark brown, large and compact, with gold hairs, and the petals are broad and rounded. Can be grown without staking at all as the stems are very wiry and strong. The only really dark blue early-flowering delphinium.

Mid-Season

'Royalist'

> *Height:* 6 ft *Length of Spike:* 2 ft 6 ins. *Diameter of Floret:* 3½ ins.
> *Raiser, Introducer:* Blackmore & Langdon *Year of Introduction:* 1951
> *Awards:* A.M.-Trials, 1953; F.C.C., 1956

The inner petals are royal blue, flushed rosy purple and the outer petals are tipped royal blue with a creamy white, yellow-haired eye. The spike is narrowly pyramidal, well-tapered, and the stems are bronze and very strong indeed. Mildew-resistance in these dark colours is only moderate.

Late

* 'Jack Tar'

> *Height:* 5 ft *Length of Spike:* 2 ft 6 ins. *Diameter of Floret:* 2 ins.–2¼ ins.
> *Raiser, Introducer:* Bishop, Bakers *Year of Introduction:* 1956

A notably attractive plant with particularly healthy foliage. The front petals are a rich cornflower-blue deepening markedly towards the edges and the eye is small and dark. The whole effect is the darkest and purest of blues, the spikes being columnar and well-formed. This plant stands alone in its season and is an extremely pure blue.

9 . VIOLET SHADES

For want of a better solution several entirely different violets have been grouped in this section, but there are as yet no early-flowering varieties available.

71. Spikes of 'Royal Marine' – see Fig. 1 and Chapter 13

Mid-Season

* 'Royal Marine'

Height: 7 ft *Length of Spike:* 3 ft *Diameter of Floret:* 3 ins.–3½ ins.
Raiser, Introducer: Blackmore & Langdon *Year of Introduction:* 1958
Awards: A.M.-E., 1957; A.M.-G., 1961

This is a bright violet-blue self, with rounded and flat florets enhanced by a conspicuous and flat eye of creamy white. The spikes are broadly pyramidal and taper finely. A lithe and strong stem.

* 'Minstrel Boy'

Height: 3 ft 6 ins.–4 ft *Length of Spike:* 2 ft–2 ft 6 ins *Diameter of Floret:* 2½ ins.
Raiser, Introducer: Bishop, Bakers *Year of Introduction:* 1957

This is the same shade of Parma-violet as 'Matchless' but is a valuable semi-dwarf with a striking black, brown, and gold eye. This colour is really a very deep heliotrope.

Mid-Season to Late

'Matchless'

Height: 5 ft 6 ins. *Length of Spike:* 3 ft 6 ins. *Diameter of Floret:* 3 ins.
Raiser, Introducer: Bishop, Bakers *Year of Introduction:* 1958

The flat, pointed petals are a rich amethyst-violet with a blending brown eye and are very well placed to form a solid and beautifully tapered columnar spike. This is a new colour in delphiniums, called by some Parma-violet, and really an intensification of the heliotrope shade.

* 'Bermuda'

Height: 5 ft 6 ins. *Length of Spike:* 3 ft 6 ins. *Diameter of Floret:* 4 ins.
Raiser, Introducer: Bishop, Bakers *Year of Introduction:* 1959

The rounded florets are perfectly formed into long and pyramidal spikes. The colour composition is extremely rich, being cobalt-violet, flushed French blue, with a conspicuous and contrasting black and gold eye, a very distinctive Commonwealth plant.

72. 'Savrola', plum-purple,
has a pleasing spike

Late

* 'Sparkling Eyes'

Height: 5 ft *Length of Spike:* 3 ft *Diameter of Floret:* 3 ins.
Raiser, Introducer: Bishop, Bakers *Year of Introduction* 1961

The front petals are of pure cobalt-violet and the tips of the back
petals are touched with cobalt-blue. The florets are round and
formal and offset by a large and perfectly formed flat, circular eye
of pure white, with light flecks of cobalt-blue. Placement is perfect
but not close and the spike is pyramidal and well-tapered.

10 . PLUM-PURPLE

This colour group comprises plum-purple, rosy purple, and deep lavender.

Early to Mid-Season

'Savrola'

Height: 6 ft *Length of Spike:* 3 ft *Diameter of Floret:* 3 ins.–3¼ ins.
Raiser, Introducer: Blackmore & Langdon *Year of Introduction:* 1959

This is a plum-purple with a small deep brown eye. It has a very well-formed pyramidal eye, tapering cleanly and the petals are flat with attractively serrated edges, the tips of the outers being of bright royal blue.

Mid-Season to Late

'Turridu'

Height: 5 ft 6 ins. *Length of Spike:* 2 ft 6 ins. *Diameter of Floret:* 3½ ins.
Raiser, Introducer: Blackmore & Langdon *Year of Introduction:* 1956
Award: A.M.-Trials, 1957

A very attractive rosy purple with royal-blue tips on the back petals and a black eye. The petals are crinkled at the edges, otherwise flat, and the stem is very wind-resistant. The spike is very broad at the base, tapering well.

Late

'Purple Ruffles'

Height: 5 ft–5 ft 6 ins. *Length of Spike:* 2 ft 6 ins.–2 ft 9 ins. *Diameter of Floret:* 3 ins.
Raiser, Introducer: Blackmore & Langdon *Year of Introduction:* 1955
Awards: H.C., 1956; A.M.-Trials, 1957

This is a strikingly individual delphinium as it has several rows of petals, all with frilled points and often with incurving to give a fully double appearance. The colour is a bright and deep rosy purple with plenty of royal blue on the back petals, there being no eye at all. The spike is extremely broad at the base, one of the broadest in fact, but it tapers to perfection. The stems are extremely strong and sturdy and, in fact, it often flowers at only 4 ft 6 ins. in height. Not the best of plants for mildew-resistance.

11 . DEEP PURPLE

There are very few plants indeed in this colour classification.

Early

* 'Sentinel'

Height: 7 ft–8 ft   *Length of Spike:* 3 ft 6 ins.–4 ft   *Diameter of Floret:* 3½ ins.
Raiser, Introducer: Blackmore & Langdon   *Year of Introduction:* 1961
Award: A.M.-G., 1958

The front and back petals are rounded and flat, reflexing as they mature; the colour is a very deep violet-purple, the deepest in cultivation, and is enhanced by the central bee which consists of a claw-like cluster of small purple and black petals. The spike is columnar, tapering cleanly to a point and the stems are slim and hard, with excellent wind-resistance.

There are no other deep purples in named varieties at this season.

Early to Mid-Season

* 'Purple Triumph'

Height: 7 ft   *Length of Spike:* 3 ft–3 ft 6 ins.   *Diameter of Floret:* 4 ins.
Raiser, Introducer: Blackmore & Langdon   *Year of Introduction:* 1958
Awards: A.M.-Trials, 1959; F.C.C., 1961

A very deep violet-purple self, but definitely not as dark as 'Sentinel'. The petals are flat and rounded and the eye is large and black, with gold hairs. The spikes are narrowly pyramidal, tapering well.

* 'Mogul'

Height: 6 ft 6 ins.–7 ft   *Length of Spike:* 3 ft–3 ft 6 ins.   *Diameter of Floret:* 3 ins.
Raiser, Introducer: Blackmore & Langdon   *Year of Introduction:* 1952
Award: A.M.-Trials, 1957

The colours of the front petals are rosy purple and the tips of the back petals are deep royal blue; the petals are round, often reflexing slightly, and their beauty is enhanced by the prominent white eye with its rosy purple stripes.

'Emir'

Height: 5 ft 6 ins.   *Length of Spike:* 2 ft 6 ins.   *Diameter of Floret:* 4 ins.–4¼ ins.
Raiser, Introducer: Blackmore & Langdon
Awards: A.M.-Trials, 1958; F.C.C., 1959; A.M.-E., 1961

Flat, rounded florets of immense size, a clear royal purple in colour, with a large central 'bee' of creamy white with purple stripes. A columnar spike, tapering cleanly. This plant gives of its best on a light soil.

Mid-Season

* 'Guy Langdon'

Height: 6 ft–6 ft 6 ins. *Length of Spike:* 3 ft 6 ins. *Diameter of Floret:* 3½ ins.–
3¾ ins.
Raiser, Introducer: Blackmore & Langdon   *Year of Introduction:* 1957
Awards: A.M.-E., 1952; A.M.-Trials, 1955.

Royal purple inner and outer petals, slightly touched royal-blue,
but overall impression royal-purple self; eye purple and white
striped, protruding and conspicuous; petals flat and rounded and
often somewhat reflexed. An enormous and spectacular spike
broadly tapering and pyramidal.

It is not suggested for one moment that varieties outside this
list are not worthy. When the first selection was made there were
ninety-two varieties in it but this was felt to be far too many for
our purpose. Of the twenty-three which were omitted all are good
plants but in my view they suffered in some respect or other by
comparison with those left in; sometimes there was a definite
fault and in some cases varieties were too alike.

Many plants included are not actually obtainable at the time
of writing, but all will be introduced as this book is published or
soon afterwards. In any case there are many years of experience
of cultivation to rely upon. As regards ease of propagation, it is
too complex a subject to go into by varieties, but the darker
shades are usually less easy to build up than the lighter. Many
varieties are splendid propagators; the best guide is really the
speed with which the price of the plants comes down year by
year. Some varieties – such as that great favourite 'Bridesmaid' –
are good propagators but throw so few shoots that stocks cannot
be built up fast. There are a number of plants like these which
understandably hold their higher prices rather longer; also, if the
nurseryman oversells a variety at the expense of his stock, and
then finds he has to build up again, that tends to keep prices up
too, as does a stock failure. The only thing that is a certain
indicator is a rapidly falling price – that can only mean that the
variety is an excellent propagator.

My list enables you to see how long a plant has been in commerce, and as regards Awards of Merit, whilst the 'A.M.-E.'
tag means an exhibition spike, the garden award, given after

73. Arthur Hunt, who is responsible for almost all the photographs in this book, is here seen admiring the variety 'Emir' at Wisley where an F.C.C. had justly been awarded

trial at Wisley, is really the more valuable for our purposes. It must be borne in mind, however, that varieties gaining 'A.M.-E.' in 1958 and 1959 have not yet had time to be judged at Wisley. Where a variety has gained the Garden Award after trial it means that it grew well at Wisley and was in good form on the day it was viewed by the Joint Delphinium Committee. No system is infallible, however, and the Committee cannot be at the trials every day. Living very near, as I do, I have seen many a good plant in A.M. form at the wrong time, so failing to obtain recognition, and, conversely, there have been a few plants which have been lucky enough to look better, at the critical moment, than they really are.

An Award of Merit after trial at Wisley is a hallmark which guides the public in selecting plants. Once recommended and given it cannot be taken away. Yet, undeniably, the keeping properties of the florets and the strength of the stems are of the highest value in the garden; it is sometimes difficult for the Joint Delphinium Committee to judge these valued qualities accurately.

As regards the Bishop and Commonwealth strains, the only two of my recommendations which have been put up for award are 'Great Britain' and 'Cinderella'. The former received an award and I have no doubt that 'Cinderella' will gain one – it only went to Wisley in 1958. My selections from Codsall have accordingly been made from personal knowledge plus experience at Codsall, and without the benefit of seeing them at Wisley alongside the others, but I do not think that they will disappoint.

Those who know their delphiniums well will doubtless notice and regret the absence of many well-known plants – for example 'Valentia', 'Mrs Frank Bishop', 'Ivy Ridgwell', 'Blackmore's Glorious', 'Dora Cairncross', 'Sir Neville Pearson'. These are all plants which will continue to give good service in the garden for many years, but in quality they have definitely been superseded.

14 · The future of the delphinium

For years now the gardening world has been sighing, somewhat illogically, for the blue rose, the yellow sweet pea, the blue dahlia, a lupin of pillar-box red, among other things. In the world of delphiniums new colours such as cream, yellow, orange, and scarlet do exist and proliferate in the wild so that hopes for garden hybrids in these shades do have some foundation.

Yellow and Cream

Yellow- and cream-coloured hybrids have occurred in seedling plantations in the U.S.A. and in Great Britain frequently for fifty years or so. All have been cursed with delicate lungs and though some, such as 'Primrose' and 'Golden Gown', have been capable of propagation and have had a period of successful cultivation, none has as yet provided the means of establishing these desirable colours in a series of plants of good constitution. The author possesses a cream-coloured seedling with healthy foliage. This is a step forward perhaps, but history shows the colour to be recessive so that breeding may lead' to nothing. Certainly it is not hopeful. And when it comes to yellow there has quite definitely never been any hybrid to approach the species *Delphinium zalil* which in its native Afghan conditions is a fine perennial fully worthy of a place in any garden. It gives a good golden yellow effect, a combination of primrose-yellow petals coupled with orange-scarlet markings on the corolla, and will probably remain unchallenged. No one has ever done any serious recorded work on this plant, yet it is the only plant which can ever hold out to gardeners any real hope of yellow garden hybrids. The wild plant itself, in a good form, has been cultivated for years by A. A. Samuelson of Washington, U.S.A., and is undoubtedly garden-worthy in suitable climates with a short hot and dry summer and a long snow-bound winter. There is nothing new in all this; it has all been known since 1885 when the naturalist Dr J. H. T. Aitchison featured it in a botanical report.

No one can deny that here is a yellow delphinium. It exists, is a common sight in the mountain valleys of Gilran, and is desirable in form and colour. It only remains for me to underline that here still is a golden opportunity which has lain before us for more than seventy years.

White delphiniums came fitfully upon the scene for many years, lacking stability, vigour, and perenniality, yet have returned in good order. All of these were originally either albinos or chance seedlings, yet permanence has been achieved. The hope for a yellow hybrid of quality is remote, but there must be a chance of producing selected forms of *D. zalil* itself which could give a creditable performance in European conditions.

Red and Pink

While no garden hybrid has ever rivalled *D. cardinale* for colour, it has been seen that red and pink hybrids do exist, though not on a sound foundation such as the blues and mauves. Scarlet exists only in the wild *cardinale*, vermilion-scarlet and orange in the wild *nudicaule*, and to grow these from seed as annuals in European conditions seems far more satisfactory than to wait for *elatum* hybrids of good constitution, any hope of which must be very remote. Frank Reinelt has put in years of work in an endeavour to take advantage of the occasional cream seedlings which often occur, and in pink and red he has succeeded in evolving the Astolat *elatum* hybrids in blush, magenta rose, and mulberry colour, though the vigour and constitution of these is suspect and the colour impermanent. The improvement of this strain in colour and in perenniality offers scope to the breeder, but will be a long and hard road.

Other New Colours

There seems little hope of new colours as such, the range being very complete. What undoubtedly is materializing, however, is new and pleasing combinations in the more delicate pastel tones. Notably a white flower with a magenta pink tone, definitely deepening on the petal edges, and various plants of a shade of softest heliotrope so delicate as to appear grey. Not to be seen at their best in the border perhaps, such plants have definite attraction in flower arrangement.

74. 'Golden Gown' had a few years of popularity in the twenties, but, as with all yellow hybrids so far, it was a losing battle; poor foliage and weak constitution won the day

A small but attractive development in pure white is also occurring. A plant is being propagated which has very pronounced green shadings on the reverse of the petals as well as green markings in the centre of the front white petals. In bud and at maturity the effect of greenness is pronounced and attractive, reminiscent of some of the white narcissi.

Double Forms

Three exist, 'Lady Eleanor', 'Alice Artindale', and 'Boningale Glory', but the best of these is the first-named and oldest. All three are a mixture of pale rosy mauve and pale blue, with 'Alice Artindale' distinctly deeper in tone. There seems room for a few more fully double rosette-like florets, although in a way they are only one of nature's mutations whereby the corolla is replaced by extra petals.

Scent

Fragrance is always desirable. Named varieties of white *elatum* hybrids which are pleasantly scented have existed since the 1930s but the modern 'White Nylon' bred by A. E. J. B. Kidney of Thornton Heath is the only named example in cultivation. Other scented seedlings exist, however, including a blue plant, so that scent in the delphinium becomes a possibility. When grown under glass for Chelsea, Blackmore and Langdon's 'Sorrento' is found to be scented also.

Bushy Forms

Fig. 76 shows florets of the new seed strain known as Connecticut Yankees, distribution of which may be shortly expected. These plants resemble *D. tatsienense* in their bushy, much-branched habit and in their floriferousness, and the colour range is known to include pale blue, sky-blue, gentian, dark blue, and purple with bees varying from white to fawn and brown. Whether this seed strain will make plants which are perennial in Europe or which will need to be grown from seed each year remains to be seen.

Market Varieties

Elatum delphiniums are sent to market as cut flowers but full

75. This Giant Pacific
    'Astolat' seedling is of
    the brightest possible
    magenta pink and is
    very vigorous – an ex-
    ception to the general
    rule for these 'pinks'

advantage of this possibility for breeding has not yet been taken. On this point Allan Langdon wrote to me as follows:

Most of the older generation of delphinium growers will remember the variety 'Nora Ferguson' which figures in the fourth generation of 'Blue Jade's' family tree. This was a variety of exceptional stamina and perenniality. Many thousands of spikes of it were sent to the country's flower markets for it had a thin, wiry stem, kept well in water, and did not easily shed its petals. Had this type of plant and its stable-mate 'F. W. Smith' been selected and used more for breeding than they were, a race of plants could have been produced which would have been invaluable to the cut-flower trade in addition to their garden value. The quest for larger and yet larger flowers, however, won the day, and this most worthwhile type of plant was left to fade away.

Public demand was for the large flowers, and breeding plans with too many facets are not practicable. Nevertheless, for the semi-dwarf *elatum* hybrids, of which we have made mention and which are discussed below, a very great success is predicted which may well point the way for the breeders to concentrate on a smaller version still which could withstand the market handling and yet give a fine display.

Existing elatum Hybrids

After reading this book, and especially after first scrutiny of the Selected List of Varieties in Chapter 13, many may think there is nothing left to be desired. But a closer study of my analysis of the best existing varieties into eleven colour groups, and each colour group into five seasons, throws into relief several clear gaps still to be filled. For instance the well-known 'Swanlake', white and with a black eye, is not really a pure white at all. It is also early to flower so that, if two pure whites were introduced with a black eye, the one early and the other late, both would be very welcome.

Then again, at Bath we have a new range of intense blues heralded by 'Mollie Buchanan', 'Greville Stevens', and 'Supermarine'. All of these are valuable late flowerers and on the tall side; apart from height, there is a real need for blues of this intensity early in the season.

From Codsall there is plenty of room for a wider range of Parma-violet such as 'Minstrel Boy', to cover the whole season,

76. Florets of this substance on bushy much-branched plants, will be welcomed when the seed of the 'Connecticut Yankees' is distributed

and for early-flowering white-eyed pure whites to complement the later-flowering 'Purity' and 'Janice'. Another want revealed in the previous chapter refers to the range of plum-purple varieties from Bath, such as 'Guy Langdon', 'Emir', 'Purple Triumph', 'Mogul', 'Sentinel', and 'Savrola', of which only the first-named is mid-season. The others are all over by mid-season and there is room for a really late-flowering version of 'Sentinel' and 'Emir'.

There is obviously room for many more varieties in the late-flowering category, and still more improvement is possible in the lasting properties of the florets. Substance of petal and the ability to hold until well after the top of the spike is open make the delphinium more and more desirable as a border plant and these are properties to which more attention should be paid when plants are being judged.

These few instances show that there is plenty of progress still to be made in existing lines of breeding. Additionally, there is the question of bee or eye variety. A change of colour and formation in the centre of a floret can transform it completely. Fawn-coloured eyes, eyes of the same colour as the petals, exotic-looking grey-coloured bees with cream edges, all are known to occur and if bred into plants of the best and most suitable colours would represent a desirable widening of choice. In California, for instance, Frank Reinelt is attempting to stabilize a pure yellow bee on a clear light blue flower. In the past he had a strain of light blues with fawn bees but had to scrap them because the plants were too big for the spikes and subject to mildew. This breeder has in fact done a great deal to increase the colour range and variety of bee, the importance of which to the whole appearance of the spike is never fully appreciated.

Semi-dwarf Plants

Several named varieties in the range from 3 ft to 4 ft 6 ins. have already been mentioned in foregoing chapters and details of all will be found in Chapter 13. All are natural mutations occurring at Bath and Codsall, except the varieties 'Blue Jade' (see Fig. 77) and 'Bebe'. If you studied the pedigree of 'Blue Jade' in Chapter 6 you will have noted that its male parent 'Blue Tit' was the mutation and that it occurred in 1952. At Bath full advantage was

77. This is 'Blue Jade', the pedigree of which is to be found on p. 124.
Altogether a delightful plant with its large and pure soft blue florets
and its moderate height of 4 ft–4 ft 6 ins.

78. 'Melbourne', one of the new Commonwealth strain, forms a particularly symmetrical spike. It is spectrum blue, shaded with heliotrope, and grows to a height of 4 ft 6 ins. only

taken of this 'break' and breeding has been going on ever since with the sole primary object of fixing the 'dwarfness' at from 3 ft to 4 ft. The three plants named are mildew-resistant, of amazing vigour and full perenniality, as are other unnamed seedlings from the same crosses. The colour range of this short-growing strain is at present in mid-blues, dark blues, and purple only. The light mauves and violets have yet to come, and new 'breaks' are rightly hoped for in each new batch of seedlings. But perhaps the factor of most value about the whole project is that seed from this collection within a collection is coming

79. A good 'Percival' seedling of the Giant Pacific strain, purest white,
jet-black in the eye and heavily spotted green on reverse of petals.
This particular plant roots and performs well from cuttings

75 per cent to 80 per cent true for height, and this despite the fact
that 'Blue Tit's' parents were 6-ft 'Royalist' and 7-ft 'Charles
F. Langdon'.

Seed of the new strain is confidently expected to be on offer in
the season 1962, together with several other named varieties
which are at present being developed. Quite clearly, at these
heights, such plants and such seed will greatly enhance the value
of the delphinium and permit its growth even in the windiest and
most exposed sites as well as in the tiniest of gardens and on
the smallest cash resources. A most noteworthy landmark in

line-breeding, the current value of which can be seen at Wisley in the special trial of semi-dwarfs which was first planted in 1959 from plants supplied by Blackmore and Langdon.

Commonwealth Seed

This strain raised by the late Frank Bishop is typified by large and mildew-resistant foliage throwing up imposing spikes in all shades of pale mauve, heliotrope, and Parma-violet coupled with great variety of bee. Seed of this new strain has not as yet been distributed and is therefore something else to look forward to in the near future. And in Commonwealth named plants we have yet to welcome the most desirable colour of all – blue, which as usual is still lagging behind the mauves.

General

Progress nowadays is made at an increasing pace. Real improvements in named plants are being introduced at a speed which was impossible before the Second World War when, as we have seen in earlier chapters, there was a race by too many breeders to name and market too many varieties in an attempt to satisfy a public crazy for size. Controlled breeding to a set of desirable standards has now come into its own and for a lesser effort in plants named a much higher standard is being achieved. With few exceptions plants cannot last in popularity more than ten years under such pressure from succeeding generations, unless they are quite exceptional.

There seems no reason to suppose that breeding progress will be less fruitful in the future. On the contrary the likelihood is that it will be more so.

Index